2nd

Social Studies

Daily Practice Workbook
20 weeks of fun activities

ARGOPREP

History

Civics and Government

Geography

Economics

ArgoPrep is one of the leading providers of supplemental educational products and services. We offer affordable and effective test prep solutions to educators, parents and students. Learning should be fun and easy! To access more resources visit us at www.argoprep.com.

Our goal is to make your life easier, so let us know how we can help you by e-mailing us at: info@argoprep.com.

- ArgoPrep is a recipient of the prestigious **Mom's Choice Award**.
- ArgoPrep also received the 2019 **Seal of Approval** from Homeschool.com for our award-winning workbooks.
- ArgoPrep was awarded the 2019 **National Parenting Products Award, Gold Medal Parent's Choice Award** and **the Tillywig Brain Child Award.**

SOCIAL STUDIES

Social Studies Daily Practice Workbook by ArgoPrep allows students to build foundational skills and review concepts. Our workbooks explore social studies topics in depth with ArgoPrep's 5 E's to build social studies mastery.

OTHER BOOKS BY ARGOPREP

Here are some other test prep workbooks by ArgoPrep you may be interested in. All of our workbooks come equipped with detailed video explanations to make your learning experience a breeze! Visit us at www.argoprep.com

COMMON CORE MATH SERIES

COMMON CORE ELA SERIES

INTRODUCING MATH!

Introducing Math! by ArgoPrep is an award-winning series created by certified teachers to provide students with high-quality practice problems. Our workbooks include topic overviews with instruction, practice questions, answer explanations along with digital access to video explanations. Practice in confidence - with ArgoPrep!

SCIENCE SERIES

Science Daily Practice Workbook by ArgoPrep is an award-winning series created by certified science teachers to help build mastery of foundational science skills. Our workbooks explore science topics in depth with ArgoPrep's 5 E'S to build science mastery.

KIDS SUMMER ACADEMY SERIES

ArgoPrep's Kids Summer Academy series helps prevent summer learning loss and gets students ready for their new school year by reinforcing core foundations in math, english and science. Our workbooks also introduce new concepts so students can get a head start and be on top of their game for the new school year!

WATER FIRE

MYSTICAL NINJA

GREEN POISON

FIRESTORM WARRIOR

RAPID NINJA

CAPTAIN ARGO

THUNDER WARRIOR

DANCE HERO

ADRASTOS THE SUPER WARRIOR

CAPTAIN BRAVERY

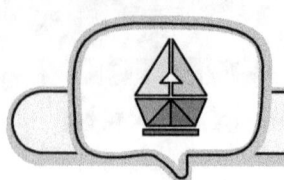

Introduction

Welcome to our second grade social studies workbook!

This workbook has been specifically designed to help students build mastery of foundational social studies skills that are taught in second grade. Included are 20 weeks of comprehensive instruction covering the four branches of social studies: History, Civics and Government, Geography, and Economics.

This workbook dedicates five weeks of instruction to each of the four branches of social studies, focusing on different standards within each week of instruction

Within the branch of History, students will make connections between their own environment and the past. In Civics and Government, they will learn more about the rights and responsibilities of citizens. Students will dive into the physical and human features of their community in Geography. Finally, in the Economics section, they will have the opportunity to learn about different jobs, good, and services.

At the conclusion of the 20 weeks of instruction, students should have a solid grasp of the concepts required by the National Council for the Social Studies for second grade.

Table of Contents

How to Use the Book

All 20 weeks of daily activity pages in this book follow the same weekly structure. The book is divided into four sections: History, Civics and Government, Geography and Economics. The activities in each of the sections align with the recommendations of the National Council for the Social Studies which help prepare students for state standardized assessments. While the sections can be completed in any order, it is important to complete each week within the section in chronological order since the skills often build upon one another.

Each week focuses on one specific topic within the section. More information about the weekly structure can be found in the Weekly Planner section.

Weekly Planner

Day	Activity	Description
1	Engaging with the Topic	Read a short text on the topic and answer multiple choice questions.
2	Exploring the Topic	Interact with the topic on a deeper level by collecting, analyzing and interpreting information.
3	Explaining the Topic	Make sense of the topic by explaining and beginning to draw conclusions about information.
4	Experiencing the Topic	Investigate the topic by making real-life connections.
5	Elaborating on the Topic	Reflect on the topic and use all information learned to draw conclusions and evaluate results.

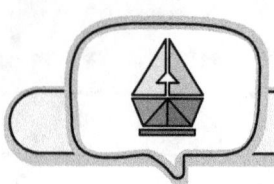
List of Topics

Unit	Week	Topic
History	1	Community Life: Past and Present
History	2	Culture & Traditions
History	3	American History
History	4	American Landmarks
History	5	Time, Continuity & Change: Recording History
Civics and Government	6	Being a Good Citizen
Civics and Government	7	Rights & Responsibilities
Civics and Government	8	Rules & Laws
Civics and Government	9	Community Leaders
Civics and Government	10	World Leaders
Geography	11	Maps & Globes
Geography	12	Travel & Transportation
Geography	13	Physical Features vs Man-Made Structures
Geography	14	Weather & Climate
Geography	15	Caring for our Environment
Economics	16	Basic Needs
Economics	17	Goods & Services
Economics	18	Producers & Consumers
Economics	19	Type of Resources
Economics	20	Jobs

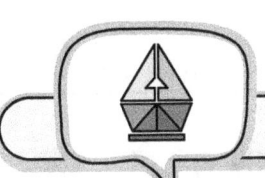

How to access video explanations?

Go to **argoprep.com/social2**
OR scan the QR Code:

WEEK 1

History

Community Life: Past and Present

Learn about the way people live together in communities and how communities change over time.

ARGOPREP

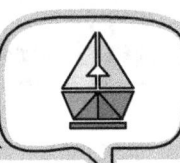

Directions: Read the text below. Then answer the questions that follow.

A **community** is a group of people living or working together in the same place. Families, schools, neighborhoods, and cities are all community groups. Each member has something in common with another. People in the same community can also be very different. This is called **diversity**. Diverse communities have people with different ways of life. They may come from different countries. They might even speak different languages.

1. What is a community?

   A. a group of people living or working together in the same place

   B. a group of people who visit different places

   C. a group of people who have nothing in common

   D. a group of people who do not speak the same language

2. Which of these groups is a community?

   A. two people who live in different countries

   B. a group of strangers visiting the same city

   C. a group of students who go to the same school

   D. one person who lives in a big city

3. _____ is when a community is made up of

   different types of people.

   A. Community

   B. Diversity

   C. Membership

   D. Language

4. Write a sentence about a community you belong to.

   _____

   _____

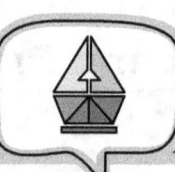
*Yesterday you learned about communities. You know that communities can be diverse. People from different **cultures** can live in the same community. Culture is the way people live. It is the way people eat, dress and celebrate.*

Directions: Read the text below. Then answer the questions that follow.

> Cultures are different all around the world. People do different activities and believe different things. Some people wear special clothes in their culture. Some families do not eat certain foods. Culture can also be a community. People who share the same beliefs are part of a culture.

1. What is culture?

    A. a town that people live in

    B. the way people live

    C. the number of people in a community

    D. a special type of food

2. True or false?

Culture is the same for everyone.

    A. true

    B. false

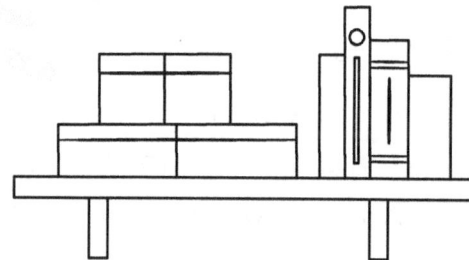

3. Write or draw 3 things from your own culture in the chart below.

food	clothing	celebrations

Directions: Read the text below. Then answer the questions that follow.

Remember that culture is not always the same. Some cultures even change over time. For example, American culture was different many years ago. People in America did not live the way they do now. They wore different clothes and survived in different ways.

The early years in America were called **colonial** times. People lived in colonies, not cities or states. They built homes with things like mud, grass, and wood. People hunted and grew their own food.

Look at the table below to see how American people lived in the past. Think about how people live differently now. Write your answer in the "present" column.

past	present
hunted and grew food	
cooked food with fire	

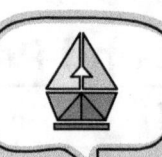
past	present
traveled by horse	
built their own homes	
wrote letters to send messages	

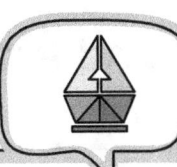
Directions: Read the text below. Then answer the questions that follow.

You know that communities and cultures change. Think about your community. This could be your family, school or neighborhood. How has it changed over the years?

Write a few sentences about your past and present community in the table.

My community in the past

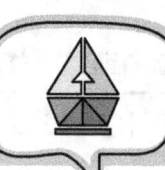
My community now

Directions: Read the text below. Then answer the questions that follow.

This week you learned about communities and culture. You know that culture can change over time. Now answer a few more questions about what you have learned.

1. Which of these is NOT a part of culture?

    A. language

    B. food

    C. height

    D. clothing

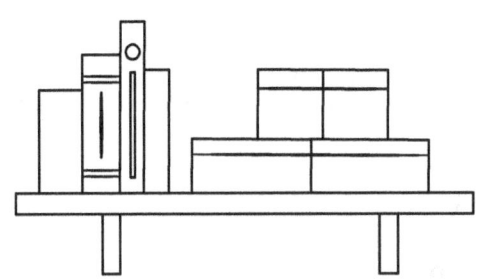

2. Which of these was used during colonial times?

    A. letters

    B. cellphones

    C. email

    D. videos

You also observed changes in your own community. Use what you learned to make a prediction. How do you think your community will change in the future?

....

....

....

....

....

WEEK 2

History

Culture and Traditions

Explore special ways people celebrate culture and history.

ARGOPREP

Directions: Read the text below. Then answer the questions that follow.

> Last week you learned about culture. You know that culture is a way of life. You also know that culture can change over time. Sometimes culture does not change. Some people do the same things for many years. These are called **traditions**.
>
> Food, clothing and celebrations can be traditional. Some cultures eat, dress and celebrate the same way on a special day. People often do this on **holidays**. These are special celebrations that happen every year. For example, Americans celebrate Thanksgiving every November. They gather for family feasts and eat traditional foods like turkey.

1. What is a tradition?

   A. a celebration that happened in the past

   B. something that people do every 10 years

   C. a part of culture that does not change

   D. a way of life that changes every day

2. Which of these is a tradition?

   A. decorating a Christmas tree every year

   B. eating a turkey sandwich for lunch

   C. a party that happened 2 years ago

   D. visiting a history museum once

3. Which of these is NOT a holiday?

   A. The Fourth of July

   B. St. Patrick's Day

   C. Cinco de Mayo

   D. Tuesday

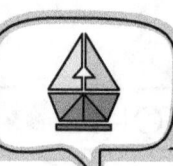
Yesterday you learned about traditions and holidays. Today you will learn more about these special celebrations.

Directions: Read the text below. Then answer the questions that follow.

There are many different holidays and traditions around the world. Look at the table below. It shows 3 important holidays and their traditions.

Holiday	Traditions	Dates
Valentine's Day	giving gifts wearing red making cards eating candy	February 14th
Chinese New Year	hanging decorations (lanterns, paintings, etc) making family dinner wearing red giving gifts	a period of 7 days between January 21 - February 20
Kwanzaa	making family dinner lighting candles in a Kinara (candleholder) giving gifts playing music	December 26 - January 1

1. On which of these holidays do people give gifts?

    A. Kwanzaa

    B. Valentine's Day

    C. Chinese New Year

    D. all of these holidays

2. Compare and contrast two of these holidays.

....

....

....

....

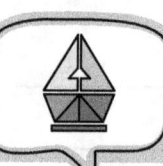
Directions: Read the text below. Then answer the questions that follow.

Hanukkah: a Jewish holiday that is celebrated in winter (November or December)

menorah: a special candleholder

latkes: potato pancakes

dreidel: a Jewish spinning top

Abigail was excited about the first night of **Hanukkah**. It was a special time for her family. She ran downstairs to help her mom light the **menorah**. Her grandmother was in the kitchen cooking **latkes**. Her brothers, Aaron and Daniel, were upstairs playing a **dreidel** game. Soon, they would all sit down at the table for a delicious dinner.

1. List 3 Hanukkah traditions from the text.

....

....

....

2. Think of another holiday that you learned about. How are the traditions different from Hanukkah celebrations? How are they alike?

....

....

....

....

....

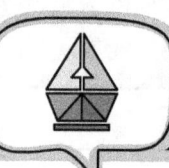
Yesterday you learned how families celebrate Hanukkah. How does your family celebrate holidays? Think about your family traditions and write them in the table below.

Directions: Read the text below. Then answer the questions that follow.

Holidays We Celebrate	Traditions

    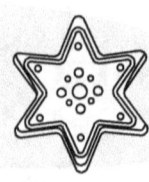

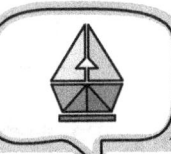
Directions: Read the text below. Then answer the questions that follow.

You've learned about several holidays and traditions this week. Remember that traditions stay the same for many years. Some of these traditions started hundreds of years ago. They were passed down from family to family.

Choose one of the traditions you learned about. Find out how it started. This is called the **origin**. You can use tools like books, videos or the Internet. Write a few sentences about what you learned below.

WEEK 3

History
American History

Learn about important American traditions and how they began.

ARGOPREP

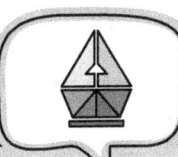
Last week you learned about traditions. You know that traditions do not change over time. You also know that traditions have origins. They started from one special day or event. People began to pass those traditions down year after year.

Directions: Read the text below. Then answer the questions that follow.

> There are many traditions in American culture. These traditions come from important events. For example, many Americans celebrate the **Fourth of July**. This tradition started on July 4, 1776. On this day, America became independent from Britain. It was once ruled by British leaders. Americans celebrated with bells, music, and parades. July 4, 1777 marked one year of freedom. This Independence Day celebration included fireworks and bonfires. Americans still follow these traditions hundreds of years later.

1. What happened on the first Fourth of July?

    A. Americans traveled to Great Britain.

    B. British rulers made new laws in America.

    C. America became independent from Great Britain.

    D. American rulers took over Great Britain.

2. The Fourth of July is also known as ....

    A. America Day

    B. Independence Day

    C. Freedom Day

    D. Great Britain Day

3. Which of these is a Fourth of July tradition?

    A. parades

    B. candles

    C. trees

    D. turkey

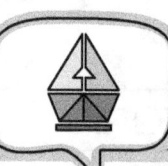
Yesterday you learned about an important American tradition. You know that people celebrate Independence Day on July 4. This tradition started in 1776. Today you will learn about more American traditions and how they started.

Directions: Read the text below. Then answer the questions that follow.

> American **symbols** are part of the country's traditions. A symbol is a picture or object that stands for something else. The American flag is a symbol of freedom. Its colors are red, white and blue. The flag has 13 red and white stripes. There is one stripe for each of the 13 colonies. It also has 50 stars, one for each U.S. state.

1. What are the colors of the American flag?

    A. red, white, and blue

    B. blue and white

    C. green, red and white

    D. white and red

2. What do the 50 stars stand for on the American flag?

    A. colonies

    B. presidents

    C. months

    D. states

What does the American flag look like? Draw a picture in the space below.

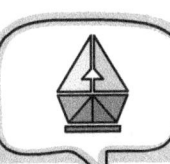
Directions: Read the text below. Then answer the questions that follow.

You know that a symbol is a picture or object that stands for something else. The American flag is an important symbol. There are many other symbols from American history.

Look at each American symbol below. Use books, videos, the Internet, etc. to find out what they mean. Write a few sentences about what you learned.

1. Bald eagle

....

....

....

....

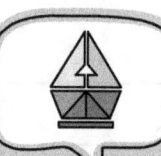
2. Liberty Bell

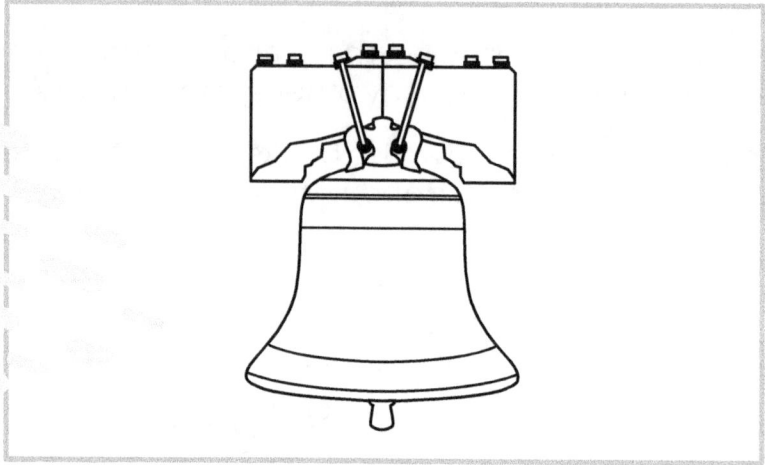

....

....

....

3. The Great Seal of the United States

....

....

....

....

Directions: Read the text below. Then answer the questions that follow.

Like symbols, songs are a part of American traditions. These songs were written many years ago. People still sing them today in America.

Have you ever gone to a baseball game? You may have heard people singing "The Star Spangled Banner." This is a traditional American song. It is sung at many events. The Star Spangled Banner is also known as the National Anthem.

The Star Spangled Banner was written by Francis Scott Key in 1814. The song is about the American Flag. Here are some of the words:

Oh, say can you see by the dawn's early light

What so proudly we hailed at the twilight's last gleaming?

Whose broad stripes and bright stars through the perilous fight,

O'er the ramparts we watched were so gallantly streaming?

And the rocket's red glare, the bombs bursting in air,

Gave proof through the night that our flag was still there.

Oh, say does that star-spangled banner yet wave

O'er the land of the free and the home of the brave!

1. How do you know this song is about the American flag? List a few keywords from the song.

....

....

....

....

2. Think of a time when you heard the Star Spangled Banner. Where were you? Why was it being sung?

....

....

....

....

Directions: Read the text below. Then answer the questions that follow.

This week, you've learned about American traditions. You know they started from important events in history. America has traditional celebrations, symbols, and songs. Today you will answer a few questions about them.

1. When did the Fourth of July tradition begin?

    A. 1492

    B. 1963

    C. 1875

    D. 1776

2. How many stripes are there on the American flag?

    A. 50

    B. 13

    C. 22

    D. 7

3. Which of these is NOT an American symbol?

    A. bald eagle

    B. Liberty Bell

    C. maple leaf

    D. flag

4. What is the Star-Spangled Banner?

    A. a song about the American flag

    B. a Fourth of July parade

    C. a book about American history

    D. an American holiday

History

American Landmarks

Explore American landmarks and find out why they are important.

ARGOPREP

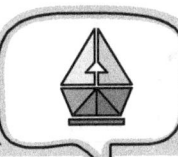
Directions: Read the text below. Then answer the questions that follow.

> Last week you learned about American history. There are many traditions and symbols that come from history. **Landmarks** are also part of American history. A landmark is a famous building or place. It has a special story about how it was made.
>
> A landmark can be a tower or a statue. It can also be a mountain or a park. In America, there are over 2000 landmarks! Some of them were built or created hundreds of years ago. Landmarks help us remember important people or events from history.

1. What is a landmark?

    A. a song about America

    B. a famous building or place

    C. an old folktale

    D. none of these

2. Which of these could be a landmark?

    A. a statue

    B. an apple

    C. a puppy

    D. an idea

3. Why are landmarks important?

    A. They help people find books about history.

    B. They protect the rights of Americans.

    C. They help people remember important people/events.

    D. They are not important parts of American history.

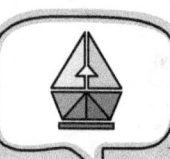
Yesterday you learned about landmarks. You know that landmarks are a part of American history. There are many landmarks in America. Today you will learn about 3 important landmarks.

Directions: Read the text below. Then answer the questions that follow.

The Statue of Liberty is a landmark in New York City. It was built in 1876. This statue was a gift from France. It was given to America to celebrate 100 years of freedom.

The White House is the home of the President of the United States. It is in Washington D.C. The White House was built in 1792. John Adams was the first president to live there.

Mount Rushmore is a famous mountain. It has four faces of American presidents. The faces were carved from stone. The presidents carved into Mount Rushmore are: George Washington, Thomas Jefferson, Abraham Lincoln and Theodore Roosevelt.

Look at each landmark. Write a fact about it on the lines below.

....

....

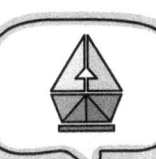
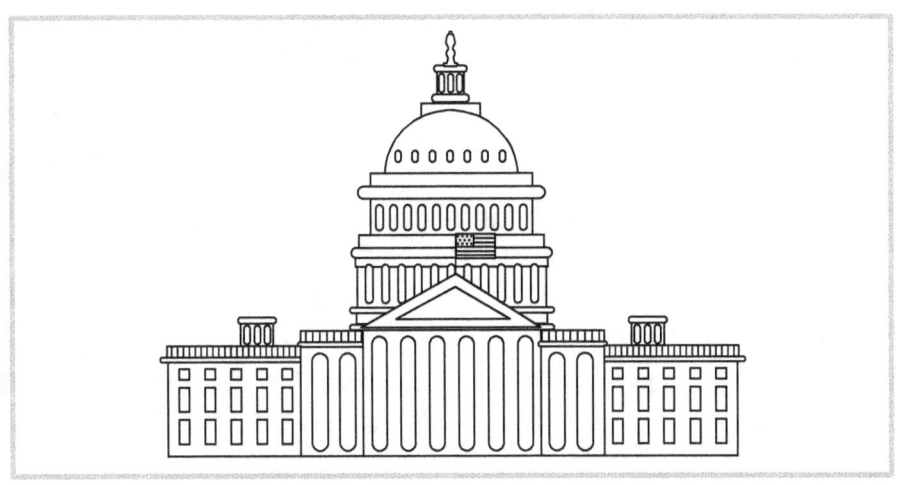

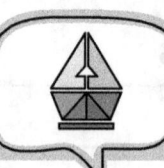
Directions: Read the text below. Then answer the questions that follow.

Remember that landmarks help us remember people and events. A **memorial** is something that honors someone who is no longer living. The Lincoln Memorial was built to honor Abraham Lincoln. Abraham Lincoln was the 16th president. His Emancipation Proclamation freed American slaves in 1862. Lincoln died in 1865.

The Lincoln Memorial took 8 years to build. It was finally finished in 1922. It is a building with a statue of Abraham Lincoln inside. Many people visit this landmark today.

1. Who was Abraham Lincoln?

_____

_____

_____

2. Why was the Lincoln Memorial built?

_____

_____

_____

3. Explain how memorials honor people who are no longer living.

_____

_____

_____

_____

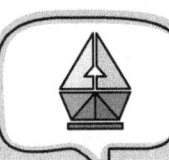
Yesterday you learned about the Lincoln Memorial. It is an important American landmark. Today you will explore another landmark.

Directions: Read the text below. Then answer the questions that follow.

Many people have **immigrated** to America. This means they moved to America from another country. Ellis Island was the first stop for American immigrants from 1892 to 1954. Over 12 million people came to America during that time!

Ellis Island is now a landmark in New York City. It is near the Statue of Liberty. Go on a virtual tour of Ellis Island at **https://www.nps.gov/hdp/exhibits/ellis/Ellis_Index.html**. You can also use books or videos. Draw a picture of what you find below. Then write a few sentences about Ellis Island.

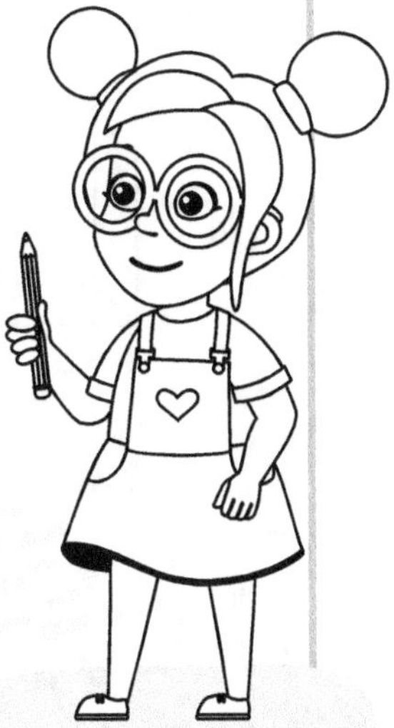

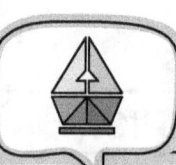
Directions: Read the text below. Then answer the questions that follow.

The Johnson family is planning a vacation. They want to visit an American landmark. The Johnsons like to see big buildings and statues. They take photos and put them in a scrapbook. They want more photos of landmarks about presidents.

Think about the landmarks you learned about this week. Which landmark should the Johnson family visit? Explain your answer below.

....

....

....

....

....

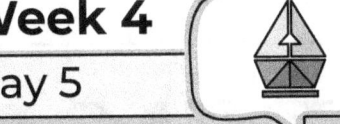
Next year, the Johnsons want to go on another trip. Mrs. Johnson wants to know more about immigrants from the early 1900s. Which landmark should the Johnson family visit? Explain your answer below.

WEEK 5

History

Time, Continuity and Change: Recording History

Learn about ways people record information about important people and events.

ARGOPREP

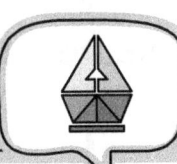
Directions: Read the text below. Then answer the questions that follow.

You've learned about history over the last few weeks. You know that some things change over time. You also know landmarks help people remember people and events. There is more than one way to remember or **record** history. Recording history helps us to have proof that something happened.

Have you ever seen an old picture? It may have shown a person who is no longer living or a house that is no longer standing. Pictures can help you see people, things, and events from the past.

There was a time when cameras did not exist. People drew or painted pictures. These pictures looked like real people and places. In 1816, people started using cameras. They could now take real **photographs**. We can still see these photographs today.

1. How can pictures help people remember past times?

   A. They can visit famous statues from history.

   B. They can show us people and events from history.

   C. They can read books about people and events from history.

   D. They can talk to people who remember events from history.

2. What is a photograph?

   A. an old painting from the 1800s

   B. a picture taken with a camera

   C. a picture that was drawn many years ago

   D. a book that was written in the past

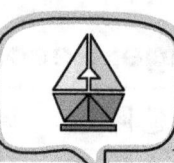
Directions: Read the text below. Then answer the questions that follow.

You have learned about ways people remember the past. You know that pictures help people see past events. Today you will learn about ways to read about history.

"
Articles are short stories about real people or events. People write articles for newspapers and magazines. These articles can be read many years later. People can learn about something which happened in the past. Read the article below.
"

Man on the Moon

July 21, 1969

Today, men have landed on the moon. At 3:56 am, Buzz Aldrin stepped foot on the moon. Neil Armstrong joined him minutes later. This is the first time humans have landed on the moon. Armstrong said, "That's one small step for man, one giant leap for mankind."

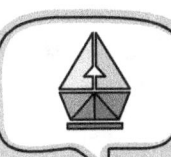
1. When do you think this article was written? How do you know?

....

....

....

2. How can this article help people learn about history?

....

....

....

....

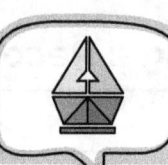

*Yesterday you learned about articles. People write articles about important events that we can read many years later. Sometimes people write about their own life. This is called an **autobiography**. When people write about someone else, it is a **biography**.*

Directions: Read the text below. Then answer the questions that follow.

Read each title below. Think about who wrote it. Circle the correct word.

My Life as the President **By Abraham Lincoln**	autobiography biography article

The March on Washington **By Time Magazine**	autobiography biography article
The Story of Helen Keller **By Jim Petersen**	autobiography biography article

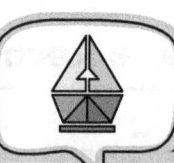
Directions: Read the text below. Then answer the questions that follow.

You know that people write about important events. Today you will write a short article. Pretend that someone will read it 100 years later. Think of something important that is happening now. How can you help the reader learn about it?

Article title:

Date:

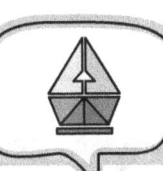
Directions: Read the text below. Then answer the questions that follow.

This week you've learned about ways to record history. People take pictures or write about events from the past. Today you will answer a few more questions.

1. How can people record history?

   A. They can take pictures with a camera.

   B. They can write about people and events.

   C. They can draw or paint pictures.

   D. They can do all of the above.

2. When people write about their own life it is called:

   A. an article

   B. a poem

   C. an autobiography

   D. a biography

3. Which of these is a biography title?

   A. All About My Family

   B. George Washington

   C. My Life Story

   D. The Battle of Gettysburg

Civics and Government

Being a Good Citizen

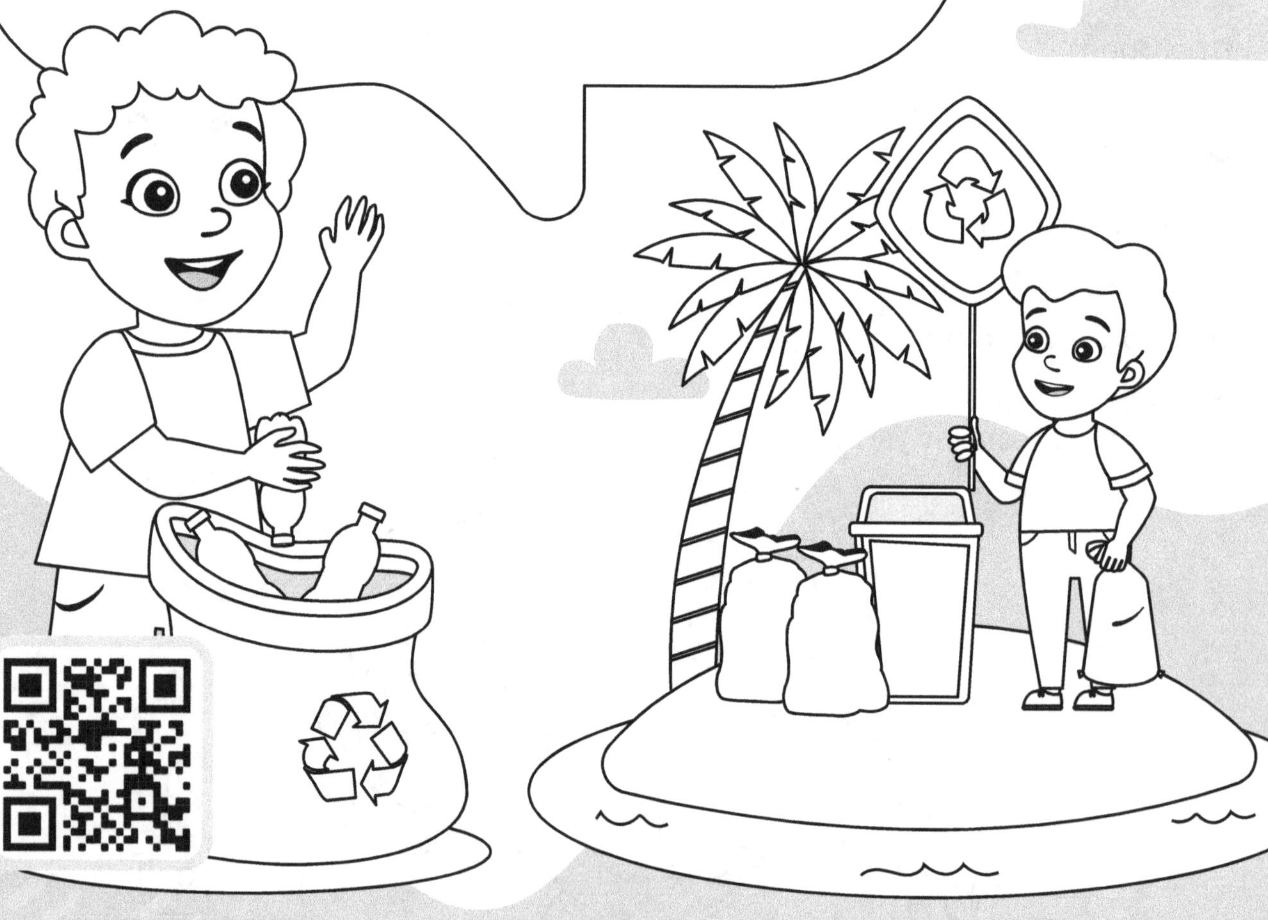

Explore ways to be a good citizen in your community.

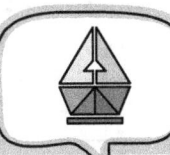
Directions: Read the text below. Then answer the questions that follow.

> A **citizen** is a person who lives in a specific place. You can be a citizen of places within your community like your school. You can also be a citizen of a city, state or country. It is important to be a good citizen which means you're doing good things for your community. You can be kind to others, follow rules and keep your community clean. Good citizens make their community a great place to live, learn or work.

1. What is a citizen?

  A. A person who likes to visit new places.

  B. A person who lives in a specific place.

  C. A person who does not follow rules.

  D. A person who is not part of a community.

2. Where can you be a citizen?

  A. on an airplane

  B. at the farm

  C. in the ocean

  D. in a city

3. How can you be a good citizen?

  A. You can do good things for your community.

  B. You can follow the laws that you like only.

  C. You can throw trash on the ground.

  D. You can ignore the school rules.

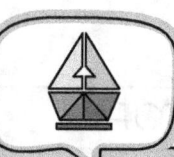
Yesterday you learned about being a good citizen. A citizen is a person who lives in a specific place. Good citizens do good things for their community.

Directions: Read the text below. Then answer the questions that follow.

You can be a good citizen in different ways. Some communities, like your classroom, are small. You can do little things like sharing with your classmates. Other communities, like the planet Earth, are very big. You (and billions of other people) can help this community by recycling and keeping oceans clean.

Look at the chart below. It shows small and large communities.

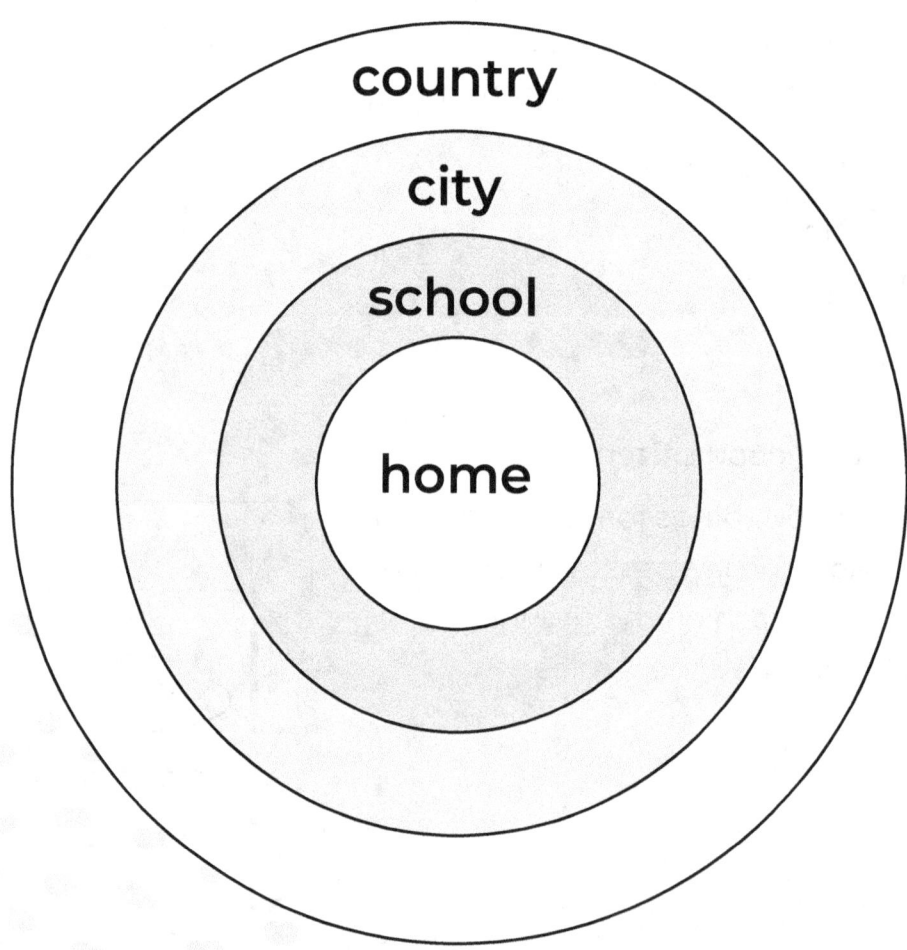

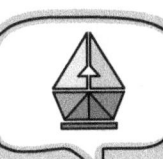
1. How can you be a good citizen in a small community?

....

....

....

2. How can you be a good citizen in a large community?

....

....

....

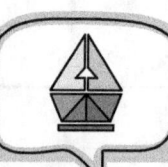
Directions: Read the text below. Then answer the questions that follow.

Jonathan lives in Los Angeles, California. He goes to school in his community. Jonathan plays on the school basketball team. He is the team captain. After school, Jonathan helps his coach clean up the gym.

On weekends, Jonathan goes to the beach. Sometimes he finds plastic bottles near the water. He collects them and recycles them. Jonathan wants the beach to be a safe place for people and animals in his community.

1. List 2 places where Jonathan is a citizen.

_____

_____

2. Explain how Jonathan is being a good citizen in his communities.

_____

_____

_____

_____

_____

_____

_____

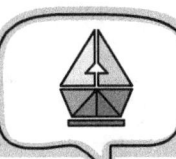
Directions: Read the text below. Then answer the questions that follow.

You have learned about ways to be a good citizen. You know that you can do good things for your community. Think about the communities you belong to. How can you be a good citizen? Fill in the chart below.

I am a citizen of... (place)	I can be a good citizen by...

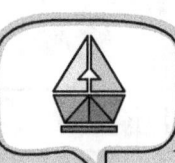

Yesterday you wrote down ways to be a good citizen in your communities. Today you will make a flyer. Pretend you want other people in your community to help you. Your flyer should show people what you want to do.

Directions: Draw your own flyer on the next page. Here are two examples below.

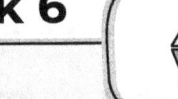
Draw your flyer in the box below.

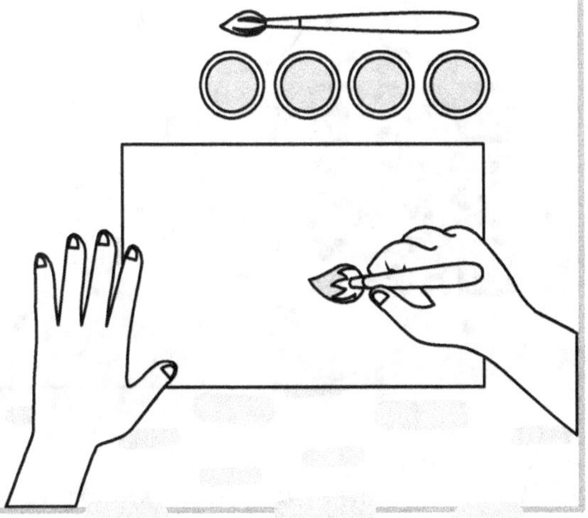

Civics and Government

Rights and Responsibilities

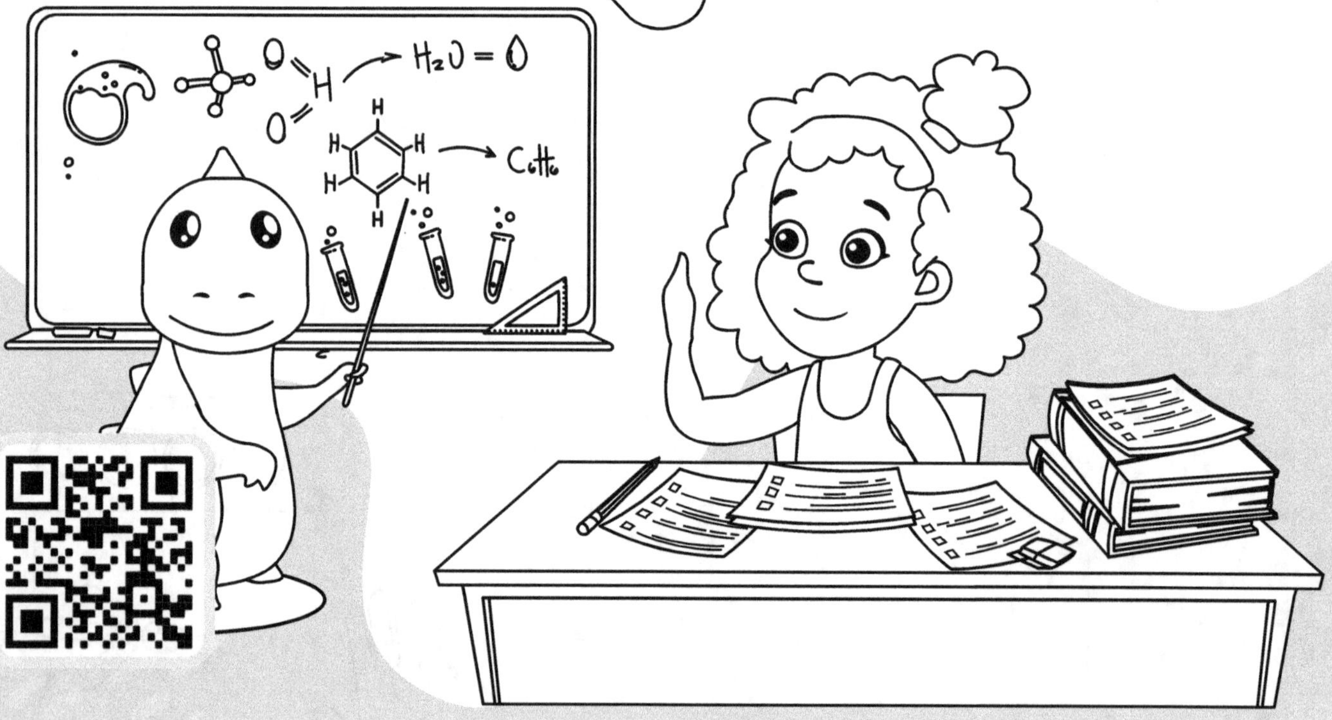

Learn about what is expected from community citizens.

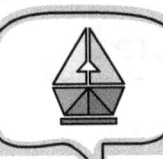
Directions: Read the text below. Then answer the questions that follow.

Last week, you learned that a citizen is a person who lives in a specific place. All citizens have special **rights**. Rights are things that you can do. For example, American citizens have the right to free speech. They can say what they think and feel about important topics.

Citizens also have **responsibilities**. These are things you must do. At school, you may have to do homework. This is your responsibility as a school citizen.

1. What are rights?

   A. Things that citizens cannot do.

   B. Things that citizens can do.

   C. Things that citizens must always do.

   D. Things that citizens should never do.

2. What are responsibilities?

   A. Things that citizens do not want to do.

   B. Things that citizens should do sometimes.

   C. Things that citizens must do.

   D. Things that citizens can do once a week.

3. True or false?

   Citizens have both rights and responsibilities.

   A. true

   B. false

Yesterday you learned about rights and responsibilities. Rights are things that citizens can do. Responsibilities are things that citizens must do. Today you will explore the difference between rights and responsibilities.

Directions: Read the text below. Then answer the questions that follow.

Look at Mrs. Garcia's class list. Then sort each item from the list in the table.

Mrs. Garcia's 2nd Grade Class

Welcome to my classroom!

1. You must arrive to class on time.

2. You can choose a book from the library.

3. You must raise your hand to ask a question.

4. You may ask for a bathroom pass.

5. All homework must be placed in the red bin.

6. You may bring your own lunch.

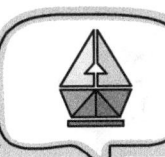
1. Choose one of the rights from the list. Why is it important?

....

....

....

....

2. Choose one of the responsibilities from the list. Why do citizens have to do these things?

....

....

....

....

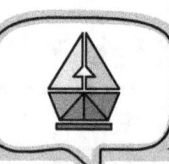
Directions: Read the text below. Then answer the questions that follow.

What are your rights and responsibilities? Think about where you are a citizen. This could be at school, in your city, or even in your country. Remember that rights are things you **can** do. Responsibilities are things you **must** do. Fill in the chart below.

I can...	I must...

Directions: Read the text below. Then answer the questions that follow.

This week you've learned about rights and responsibilities. Today you will answer a few more questions.

1. Which of these is a responsibility?

   A. You may ride your bike.

   B. You can have a slice of cake.

   C. You must do your chores.

   D. You should buy candy.

2. What is the Bill of Rights?

   A. a list of rights for American citizens

   B. a list of rights for people all over the world

   C. a list of responsibilities for American citizens

   D. none of these

3. Which of these is a right for American citizens?

   A. the right to free cars

   B. the right to steal money

   C. the right to ignore laws

   D. the right to a fair trial

WEEK 8

Civics and Government

Rules and Laws

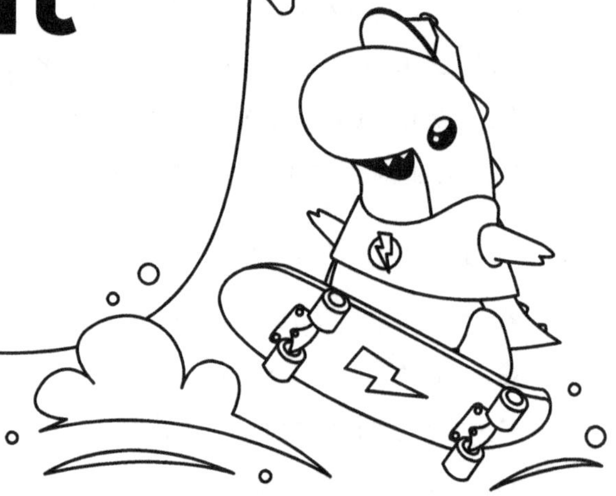

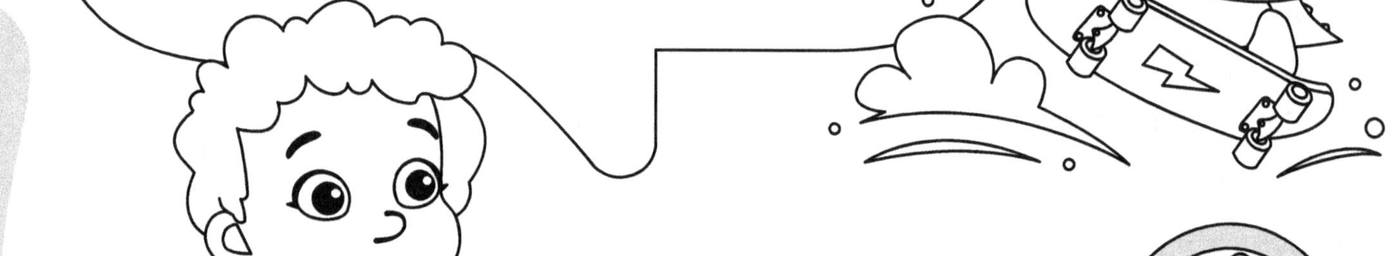

Compare/contrast rules and laws and explain why they are important.

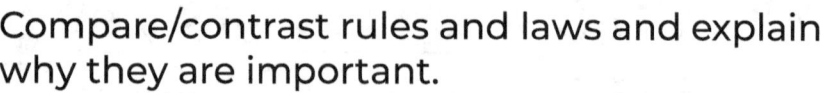

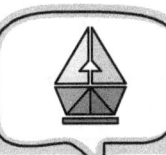
Directions: Read the text below. Then answer the questions that follow.

> Last week you learned that all citizens have rights and responsibilities. Citizens must also follow **rules** and **laws**. Rules and laws are not the same. You may have to follow rules at home or at school. Rules tell you what you should or should not do. Laws are like rules, but they are made by **government** leaders. Leaders in your city, state or country make these laws. If people do not follow laws, they may have to pay a fine or go to jail.

1. Where might you have to follow rules?

   A. at school

   B. at home

   C. in your community

   D. all of these places

2. Who makes laws?

   A. teachers from your school

   B. your parents at home

   C. leaders in your city

   D. friends in your community

3. True or false?

   Rules and laws are the same.

   A. true

   B. false

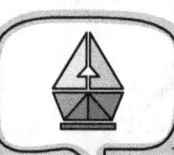
Yesterday you learned about rules and laws. You know that rules are things that you should or should not do. Laws are made by government leaders. Today you will look at signs. You may see these signs in your community. Think about what the sign shows. Is it a rule or a law? Write the correct answer on the line.

Directions: Read the text below. Then answer the questions that follow.

_____

_____

_____

_____

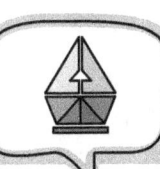
Directions: Read the text below. Then answer the questions that follow.

You know that all citizens must follow rules and laws. Rules and laws help people in the community to stay safe. Without them, people might hurt themselves or others. Look at each rule/law. Explain how it keeps people safe on the line below.

1. No diving into the community pool.

....

....

....

2. Wash your hands before dinner.

....

....

....

3. Look both ways before you cross the street.

....

....

....

4. No dogs allowed in the store.

....

....

....

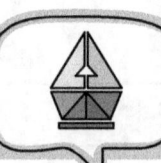
Directions: Read the text below. Then answer the questions that follow.

Think about 3 rules and/or laws that you must follow every day. Write them in the space below.

1. ....

....

....

2. ....

....

....

3. ....

....

....

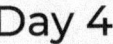

Explain why these rules/laws are important.

....

....

....

....

....

....

....

....

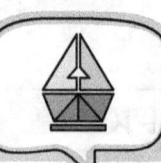
Directions: Read the text below. Then answer the questions that follow.

It was a nice spring day. Joey and Zack rode their skateboards to the park. They loved skateboarding. But when they made it to the park, they saw a new sign. It said: No skateboards allowed. Joey and Zack were sad. They really wanted to bring their skateboards to the park.

"I guess we should go back home," said Joey. "We can't ride our skateboards here."

"Well, why not?" said Zack. "It's just a silly sign. I say we ride our skateboards anyway. No one will ever know."

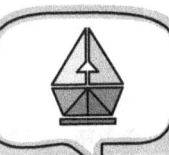
1. What do you think Joey and Zack should do? Explain your answer.

....

....

....

....

....

....

....

....

....

Civics and Government

Community Leaders

 Identify community leaders and their responsibilities.

1. Who makes treaties with other countries?

   A. mayor

   B. governor

   C. president

   D. none of these

2. Who oversees community departments?

   A. mayor

   B. governor

   C. president

   D. all of these

3. Who can veto laws?

   A. mayors

   B. governors

   C. presidents

   D. governors and president

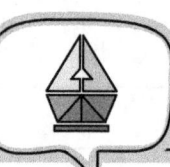
Yesterday you learned about what government leaders do. Today you will learn about how these leaders are chosen.

Directions: Read the text below. Then answer the questions that follow.

> People in the community can **vote** for new leaders. They will choose from a small group of people who want to lead them. People put their votes on a **ballot**. The ballot may be on a piece of paper or on a computer. The votes are counted. The person with the most votes is elected as the new leader.

Look at the pictures on the next page. Put them in order to show how voting works. Write the correct number on each line below.

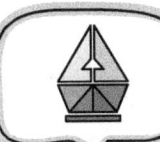

....

....

....

....

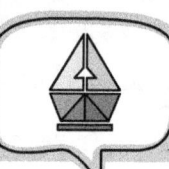
Directions: Read the text below. Then answer the questions that follow.

You have learned about community leaders this week. Who are the leaders where you live? Find out who leads your city, state and country. Write it on the lines below.

my city/town ....

my mayor ....

my state ....

my governor ....

my country ....

my president ....

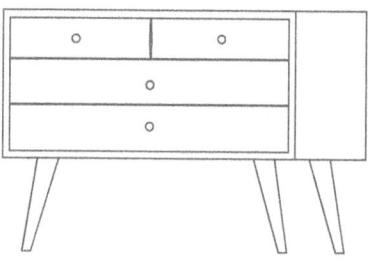

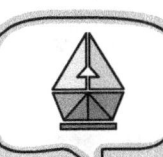
Directions: Read the text below. Then answer the questions that follow.

Leader #1 is making state laws. He vetoes the laws he believes are not good. Leader #2 oversees the city's water department. She also chooses how much money will be spent on schools. Leader #3 is the leader of a big country. He just made a treaty with France.

Think about what each leader does. Write *mayor*, *governor* or *president* on each line below.

Leader #1 ....

Leader #2 ....

Leader #3 ....

Civics and Government

World Leaders

Explore various types of leaders around the world.

ARGOPREP

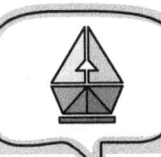
Directions: Read the text below. Then answer the questions that follow.

Last week you learned about community leaders. You know that presidents lead countries. Some countries have other types of leaders. Today you will learn about them.

Countries such as India and Canada have a **prime minister**. Like a president, the prime minister leads the country. He or she makes choices for the people and oversees the government. The United Kingdom is led by a prime minister, but it also has **kings** and **queens** as leaders who work together with the prime minister.

1. Which of these leaders is like a prime minister?

   A. mayor

   B. president

   C. governor

   D. all of these

2. Which of these countries is led by a prime minister?

   A. America

   B. Canada

   C. Mexico

   D. Russia

3. Who helps to lead the United Kingdom?

   A. mayor

   B. president

   C. queen

   D. governor

Yesterday you learned about types of world leaders. Some countries are led by presidents. Other countries are led by prime ministers or kings and queens.

Directions: Read the text below. Then answer the questions that follow.

Look at the chart below. Find out which type of leader each country has. Write the answers in the chart.

country	type of leader
Japan	
Sweden	

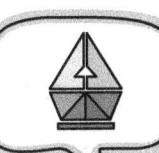
country	type of leader
Mexico	
Italy	

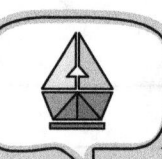
Directions: Read the text below. Then answer the questions that follow.

You know that countries can be led by different types of leaders. Today you will learn about leaders of the past.

> Many years ago, **emperors** ruled China. An emperor could rule for many years. The emperor Kangxi was the leader of China for 61 years. When an emperor died, his son became the new emperor. Puyi Qing was the last emperor of China until 1912. Today, China is led by a president. The Chinese people now vote for their president.

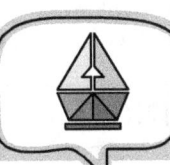
Think about how Chinese emperors and presidents are alike/different. Compare and contrast them in the chart below.

alike	different

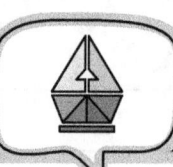
Yesterday you learned about leaders of the past. You know that China was once ruled by emperors but is now led by a president. Who leads the country where you live? How was the country led in the past?

Directions: Read the text below. Then answer the questions that follow.

Find out who the leader of your country was 100 years ago. Write a few facts about them in the space below.

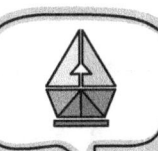
Directions: Read the text below. Then answer the questions that follow.

You have learned about world leaders this week. Today you will answer a few more questions.

1. Who can lead a country?

   A. prime minister

   B. king

   C. president

   D. all of these

2. Who led China until 1912?

   A. presidents

   B. emperors

   C. prime ministers

   D. queens

3. True or false?

   Only kings and queens can lead in the United Kingdom.

   A. true

   B. false

WEEK 11

Geography
Maps and Globes

Discover the world with geography tools such as maps and globes.

ARGOPREP

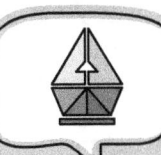
Directions: Read the text below. Then answer the questions that follow.

> You have learned that there are small and large communities. You can use tools like **maps** and **globes** to help you find them. A map is a flat picture that shows a place or parts of a place. A globe is like a round map. It is shaped like a sphere. A globe shows the whole Earth.
>
> What if you need to find a road nearby? You could use a city map. Maps are good for finding places in smaller communities. Globes show all the land and water on Earth. You can use a globe to find a world ocean or a large place like Africa.

1. What is a map?

   A. a round picture of the Earth

   B. a flat picture that shows a place

   C. a round picture of a small town

   D. a flat picture of a person

2. What does a globe look like?

   A. a cube

   B. a rectangle

   C. a sphere

   D. a triangle

3. When should you use a map?

   A. to find places in your community

   B. to see a round map of the Earth

   C. to learn about your country's history

   D. to find out how many people live in France

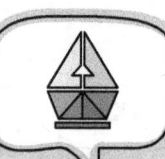
Yesterday you learned about maps and globes. You know you can use maps to find places in your community. Today you will practice using a community map.

Directions: Read the text below. Then answer the questions that follow.

> Community maps show places nearby. They also show you how to get from one place to another. You can see which streets or roads you should take.
>
> Some maps have a compass rose. The **compass rose** shows four directions: north, east, south and west. It helps you figure out which direction you should go.

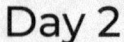

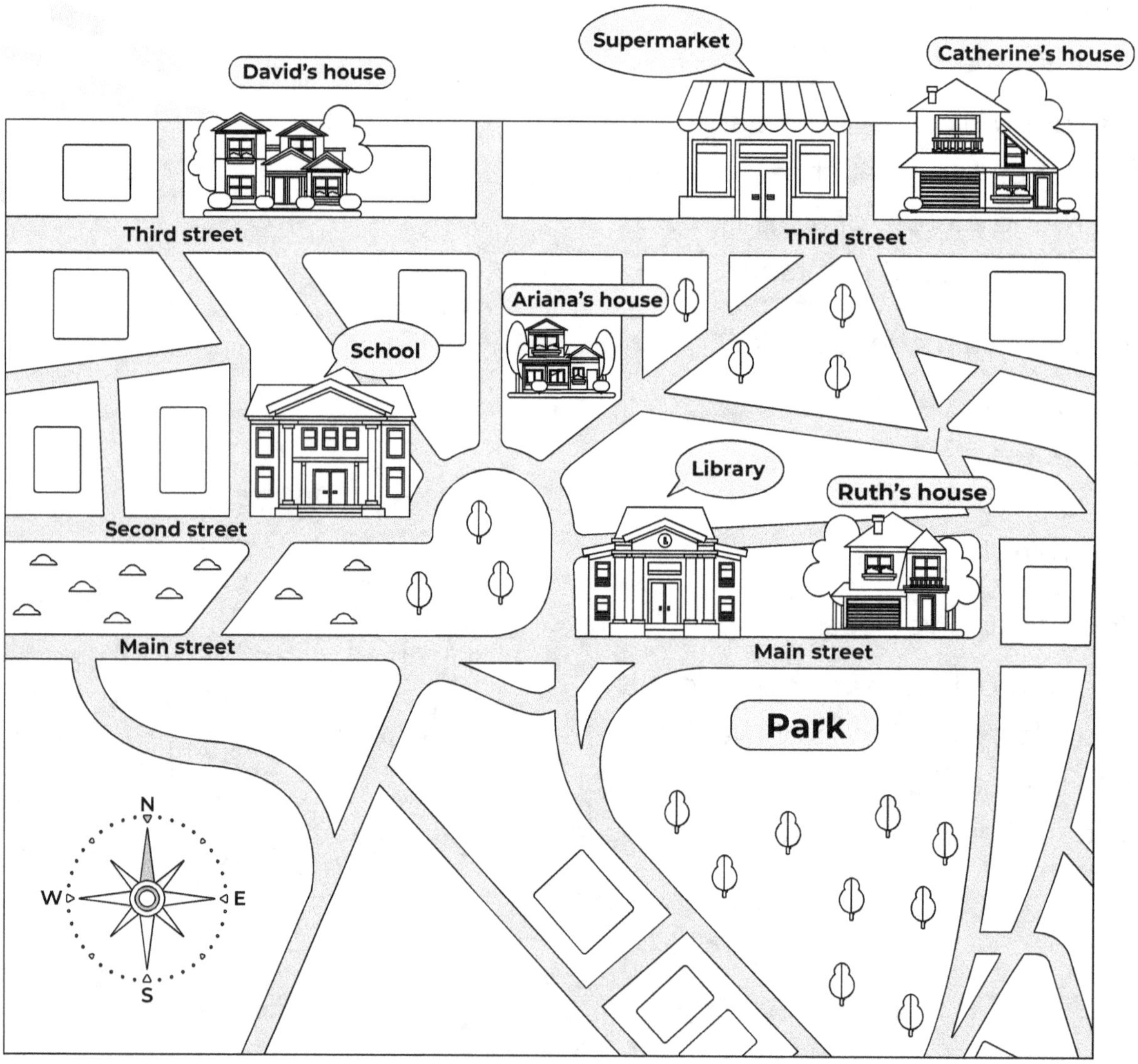

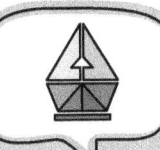
1. List 3 places that you can find on this map.

....

....

....

....

2. Explain how this map can help you get from one place to another.

....

....

....

....

Directions: Read the text below. Then answer the questions that follow.

> Remember that globes show a picture of land and water on Earth. Land is the part of the Earth that is not covered by water. A **continent** is a very large area of land. There are 7 continents on Earth. The continents have **oceans** around them. Oceans are large bodies of water.

Look at the globe below. It shows continents and oceans. Color the land green. Color the water blue.

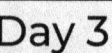

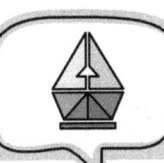
Directions: Read the text below. Then answer the questions that follow.

You've learned about community maps and world globes. Today you will think about how you might use them. Look at the chart below. Read each question on the left. What would you use to find the answer? Write *map* or *globe* in the box on the right.

How can I get from my school to the library?	
Where is the Atlantic Ocean?	

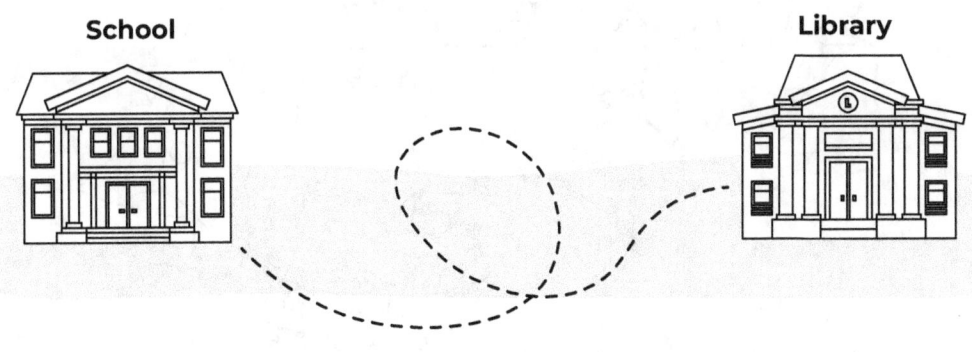

School   Library

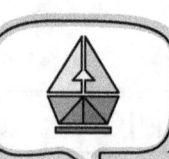
Where is the continent of Asia?	
Which street should I take to go to the park?	

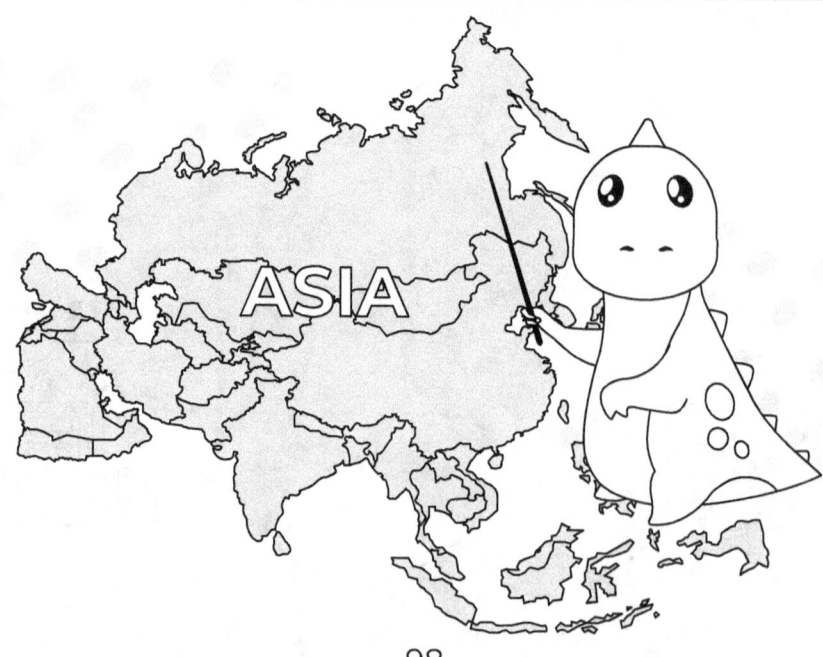

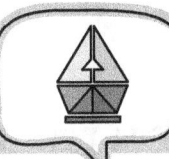
Directions: Read the text below. Then answer the questions that follow.

You have learned about maps this week. Today, you will draw your own map. Remember that a map should help you get from one place to another. You can draw a map of a small place like your house or a larger community like your city.

Draw your map in the space below.

1. How could this map help someone find their way around?

....

....

....

WEEK 12

Geography
Travel and Transportation

Explore different ways to get from one place to another.

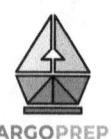

ARGOPREP

Directions: Read the text below. Then answer the questions that follow.

Last week you learned about maps. Maps can help people get from one place to another. Today you will learn about more ways to travel. Communities have **transportation** systems that help people travel.

How do you travel in your community? You might ride a school bus or take a train ride. Your parents may drive you to the community mall. Busses, trains and cars are types of transportation. People need them in order to travel.

1. What is transportation?

   A. a small town that people travel to
   B. a type of map that people use to travel
   C. someone who likes to travel
   D. a system that people use to travel

2. Which of these is a type of transportation?

   A. bus
   B. globe
   C. ocean
   D. none of these

3. Which of these is NOT a type of transportation?

   A. train
   B. building
   C. school bus
   D. car

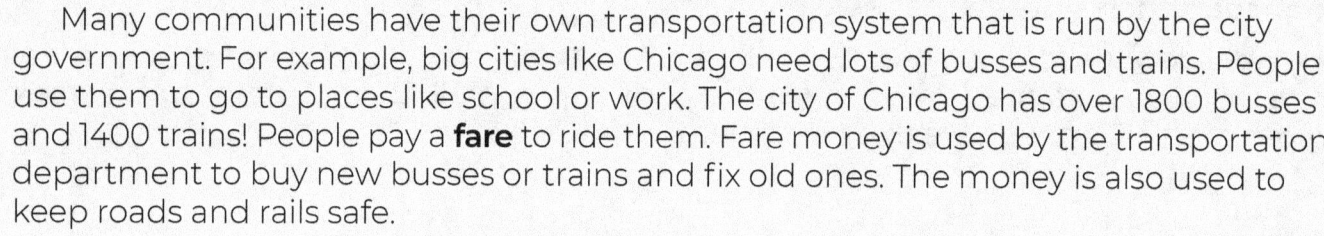
Yesterday you learned about transportation. People use transportation to get from one place to another. Today you will learn more about transportation systems.

Directions: Read the text below. Then answer the questions that follow.

> Many communities have their own transportation system that is run by the city government. For example, big cities like Chicago need lots of busses and trains. People use them to go to places like school or work. The city of Chicago has over 1800 busses and 1400 trains! People pay a **fare** to ride them. Fare money is used by the transportation department to buy new busses or trains and fix old ones. The money is also used to keep roads and rails safe.

1. Who runs community transportation systems?

    A. city government departments

    B. the president

    C. people in the community

    D. all of these

2. About how many busses are there in Chicago?

    A. 90

    B. 175

    C. 1800

    D. 12,500

3. What is a fare?

    A. a type of train that people can ride

    B. money that people pay to ride the bus or train

    C. the person who drives the bus or train

    D. a type of transportation system

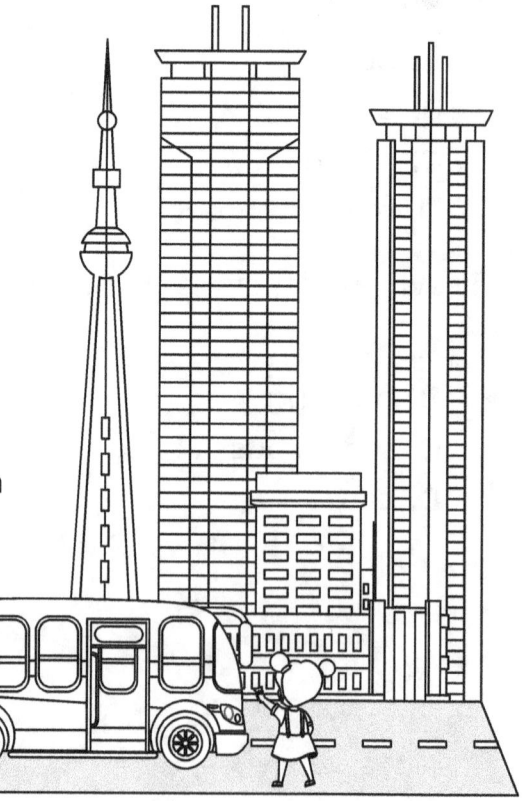

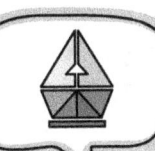
Directions: Read the text below. Then answer the questions that follow.

You know that people need transportation systems. They can ride busses and trains in the community. Some people use other types of transportation. Many people use their own cars to travel. Some people ride their bikes or they walk.

People use transportation in different ways. Busses or trains may be the best way to take long rides. They can help people save money on gas for their cars. Walking is a good way to exercise. Bike riding can be a fun hobby.

Look at the chart below. Think about why people might use each type of transportation. Write the reason in the box on the right.

transportation type	reason
train	
bike	

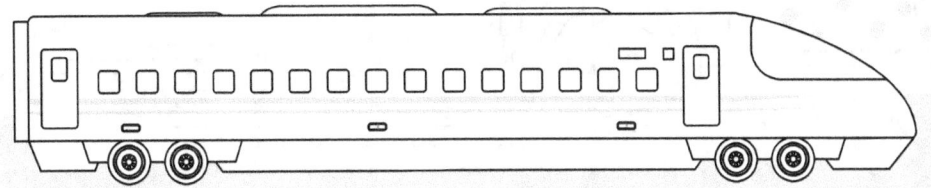

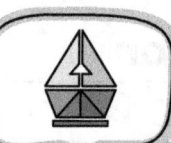
transportation type	reason
walking	
car	

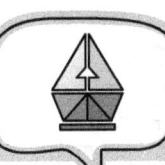
Yesterday you learned about different types of transportation. Today you will think about how you travel in your community.

Directions: Read the text below. Then answer the questions that follow.

1. How do you travel to school? Is your school close to your home or far away?

....

....

....

2. Does your family have a car? Why or why not?

....

....

....

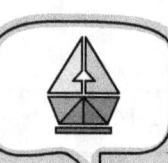
3. Have you ever ridden a train? Where did you go?

....

....

....

4. What is your favorite type of transportation? What do you like about it?

....

....

....

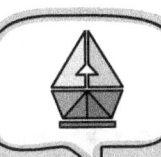
Directions: Read the text below. Then answer the questions that follow.

This week you've learned about types of transportation. You know how people travel in their communities. There are many ways to travel. The 3 main ways are by air, water, or land.

Think about ways that people can travel by air, water, or land. Write some examples in the chart below.

air	
water	
land	

Geography

Physical Features vs Man-Made Structures

Identify things that were formed by nature or were made by people.

ARGOPREP

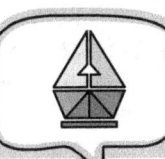
Directions: Read the text below. Then answer the questions that follow.

> Last week, you learned about transportation. There are many ways to travel. People build structures to help them travel. A structure is a building or object made from several parts.
>
> Bridges and railroads are structures. They help people travel.
>
> Bridges make it easy to travel over large areas below. They can be built over water or land. People can walk or drive across the bridge safely. Some roads have bridges above them. These roads can be used for **freight** travel. Food, packages, etc. are carried by trucks. Trains can also be used to carry freight. People build railroads to make this travel easier.

1. What is a structure?

   A. a large body of water

   B. something that is built

   C. someone who travels

   D. a type of train

2. Which of these is a structure?

   A. a river

   B. a bridge

   C. a bus driver

   D. a tree

3. How can structures help people travel?

   A. they can allow us to drive over large areas of water

   B. they can allow us to walk over large areas of land

   C. they can help trains and trucks carry freight

   D. all of these

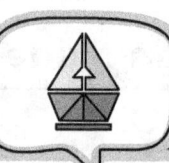
*Yesterday you learned about structures. You know that structures help people travel. Structures are **man-made.** They do not come from nature. They must be built. Today you will learn about the Golden Gate Bridge. It is a man-made structure.*

Directions: Read the text below. Then answer the questions that follow.

> The Golden Gate Bridge was built in the 1900s. People wanted a quicker way to travel to and from San Francisco. The bridge was built over a large body of water. It made it easier to drive than to travel by boat or ferry.
>
> The Golden Gate Bridge is almost 2 miles long! Millions of people drive across the bridge daily. It is also a landmark. People come from all over the world to visit the Golden Gate Bridge.

1. Why was the Golden Gate Bridge built?

....

....

....

2. How does the Golden Gate Bridge help people travel?

....

....

....

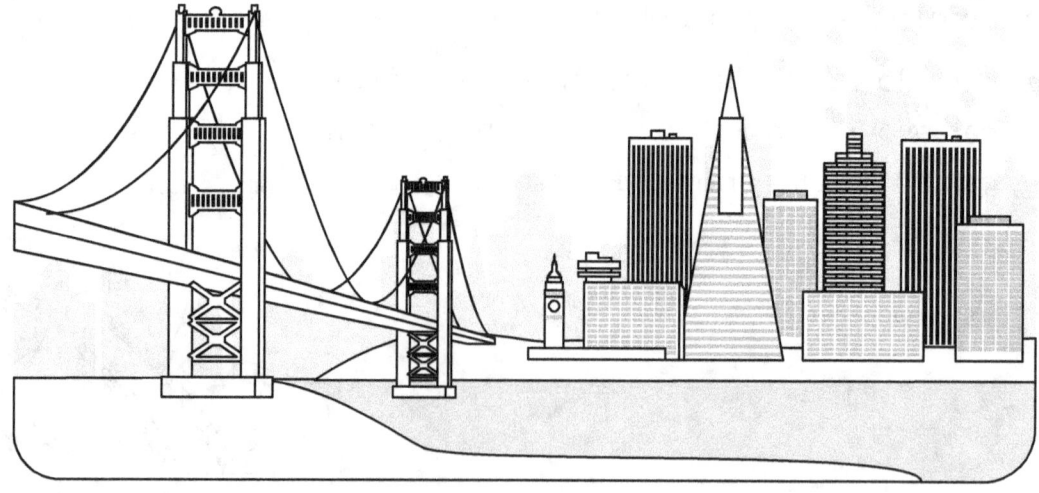

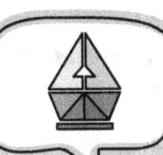
Directions: Read the text below. Then answer the questions that follow.

Remember that man-made structures are built by people. Some things are made by nature. These are Earth's **physical features**. Look at the table below. Learn more about how physical features are formed.

physical feature	how it is formed
mountain	layers of rock move upward from the Earth
hill	rocks, soil or sand get pushed into a pile by nature (wind, water, etc.)
river	a small stream of water moves and collects more water

1. Explain how physical features are made by nature.

....

....

....

....

....

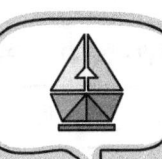
Directions: Read the text below. Then answer the questions that follow.

You know that physical features are made by nature. Look around your community. Do you see any physical features? Draw a picture of one below.

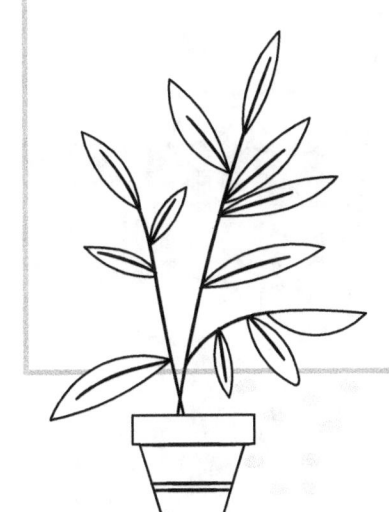

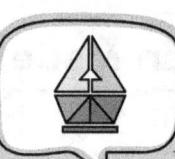
1. What did you draw? How was it made by nature?

....

....

....

....

....

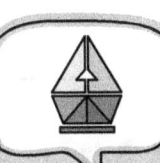
Directions: Read the text below. Then answer the questions that follow.

You've learned about man-made structures and physical features. Remember that people build structures. Physical features are made by nature.

Look at the word bank below. Sort them in the table.

river	hill	bridge
road	mountain	railroad

physical features	man-made structures

Geography
Weather and Climate

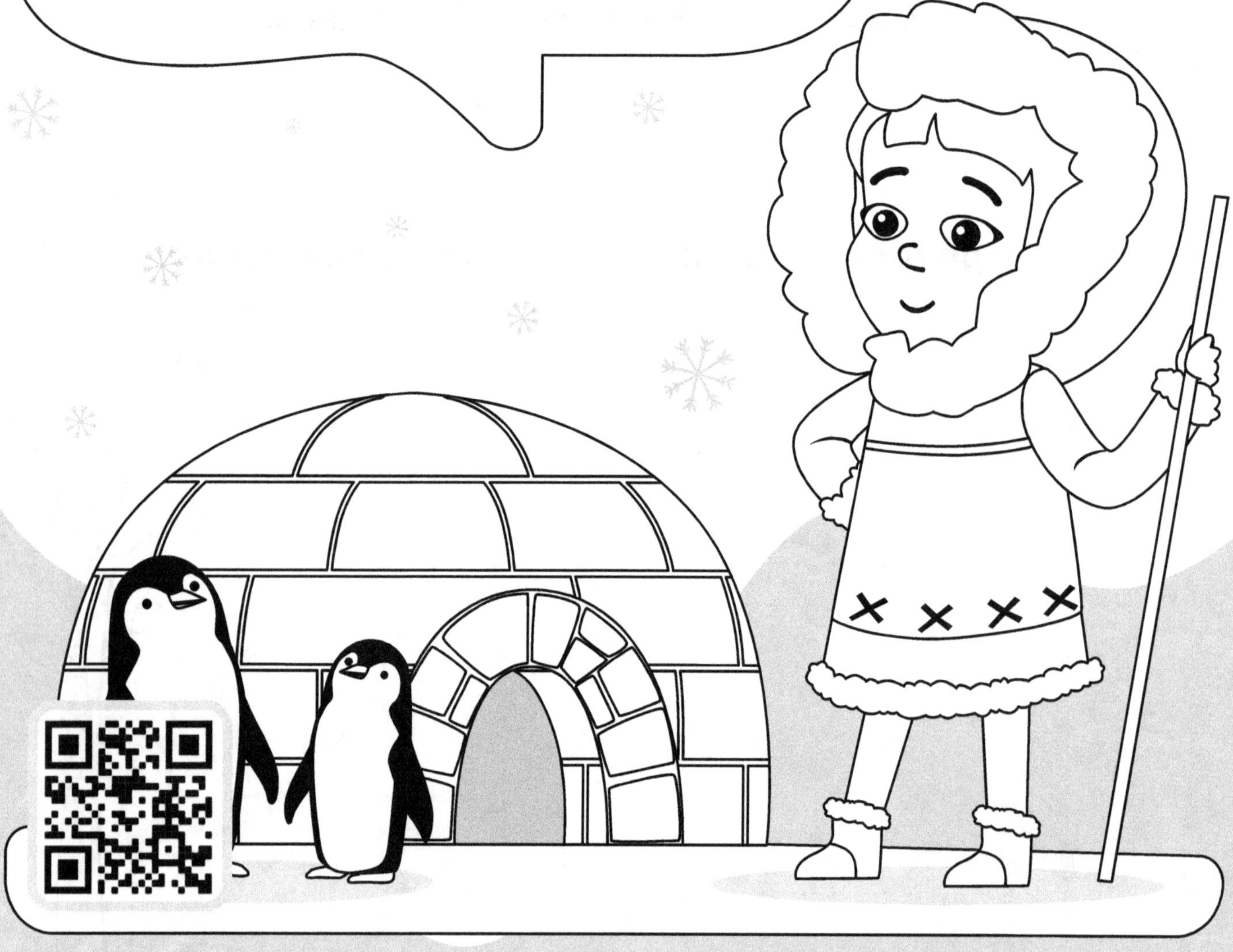

Explore how weather causes changes on the Earth.

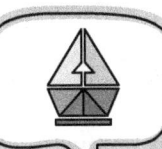
Directions: Read the text below. Then answer the questions that follow.

Last week, you learned about physical features. You know they are made by nature. Wind and rain can form hills and rivers. This week you will learn more about **weather**. Weather can make changes on the Earth. It can make places hot, cold, dry or wet.

Look outside your window. What is the weather like? The sky is part of the weather. You may see clouds or raindrops. The air around you is also part of the weather. The air might feel warm. This warmth comes from the sun. Sometimes the weather is cold. There is not much heat from the sun on cold days.

1. Which of these is a part of the weather?

    A. the sky and air outside

    B. the people inside your house

    C. the trees at a nearby park

    D. the size of your community

2. The weather can make places ....

    A. smaller

    B. far

    C. warm

    D. man-made

3. True or false?

Weather can make changes on the Earth.

    A. true

    B. false

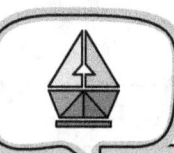

Yesterday, you learned about weather. Today, you will learn more about the effect of weather on communities.

Directions: Read the text below. Then answer the questions that follow.

> Weather can cause changes in the way people live. People can go to the beach in warm areas. In cold, snowy areas, they might go skiing. It rains often in some communities, which can cause **floods**. A flood is an overflow of water. Floods can cause the loss of homes and farms.

Think about how weather causes changes in communities. Write the cause and effect on the lines below.

Example:

cause: The sun makes the area warm.

effect: People go to the beach.

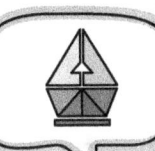
cause: ....

effect: ....

cause: ....

effect: ....

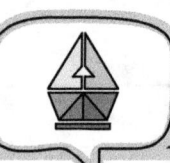
Directions: Read the text below. Then answer the questions that follow.

> Remember that weather causes changes on Earth. The weather is not the same everywhere. Some places are always warm. Some places are always cold. **Climate** is the common weather of a place. It is the weather which is there most or all of the time.

Look at the table below. Find the climate for each place. You can use books or the Internet. Write the answer in the box on the right.

place	climate
Florida	

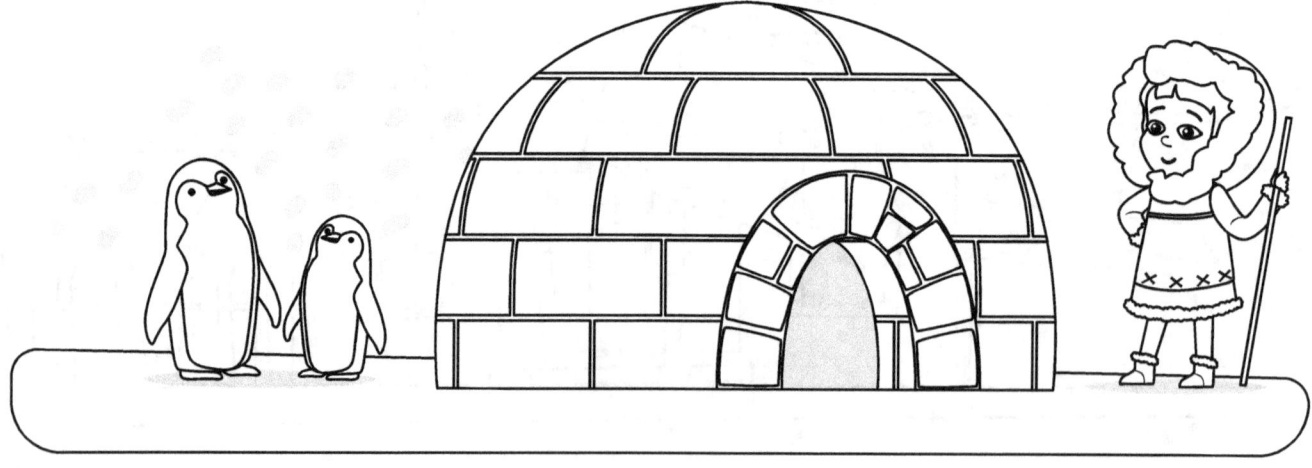

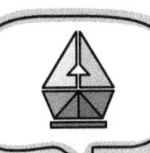
place	climate
Alaska	
Columbia (South America)	

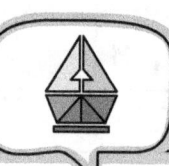
Yesterday you learned about climate. Some places have the same weather all the time. Where do you live? What is the climate there? Write it below.

Directions: Read the text below. Then answer the questions that follow.

I live in: ....

....

....

The climate is: ....

....

....

....

Today the weather is: ....

....

....

....

Directions: Read the text below. Then answer the questions that follow.

This week you've learned about weather and climate. Today you will answer a few more questions.

1. How can weather cause changes in communities?

   A. weather can change the way people live
   B. people can make the weather change
   C. weather never cause changes
   D. all of these

2. What is a flood?

   A. a lack of water
   B. a snowstorm
   C. a type of cloud
   D. an overflow of water

3. .... is the common weather of a place.

   A. flood
   B. Earth
   C. climate
   D. warmth

Geography

Caring for our Environment

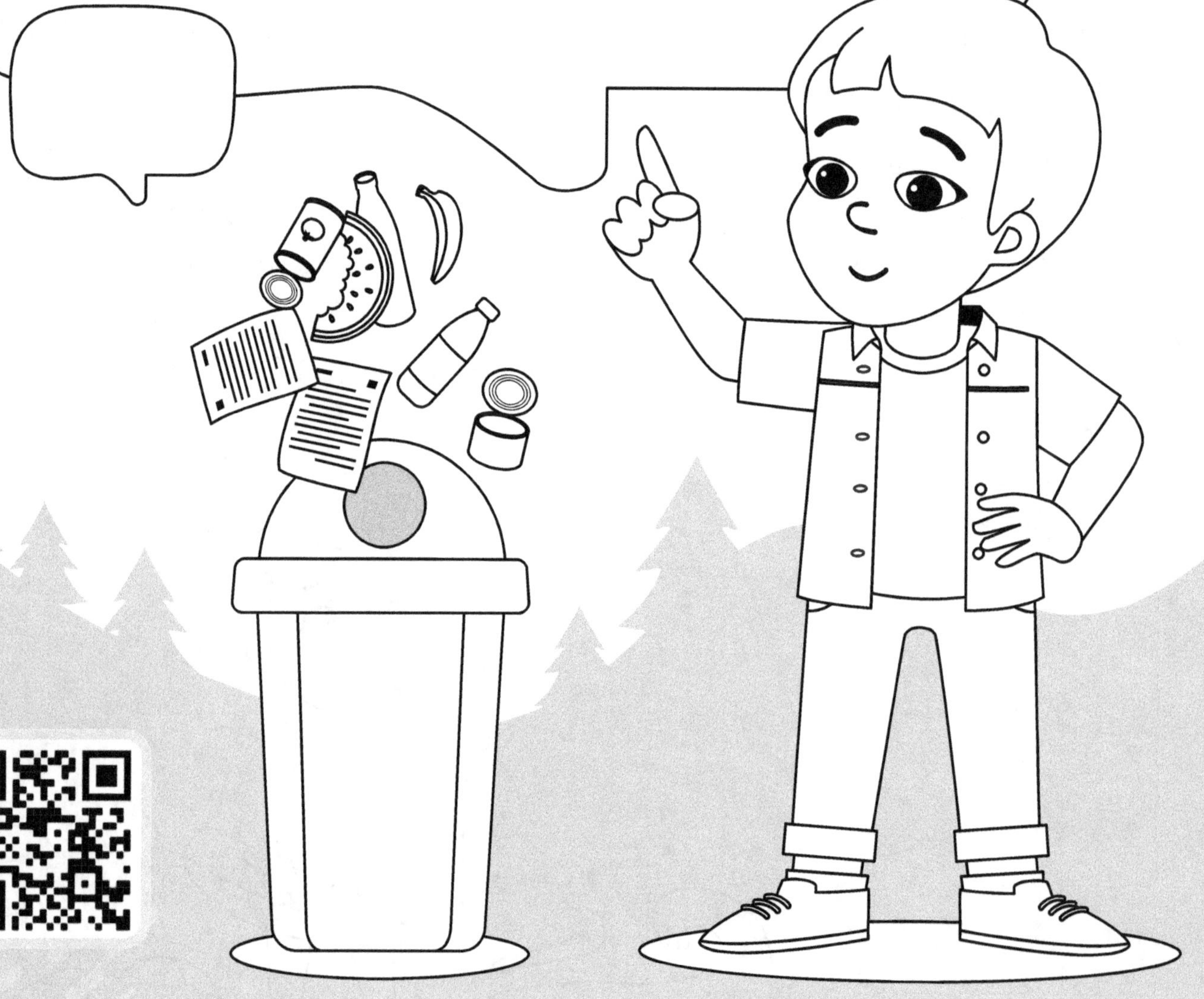

Learn about ways to keep your community clean and safe.

ARGOPREP

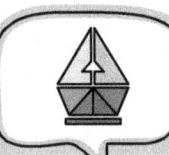
Directions: Read the text below. Then answer the questions that follow.

Remember that weather can cause changes. Some of these changes are not good. You know that floods can cause loss. People can lose their farms, homes or belongings.

Droughts are also bad for the community. A drought is when there is not enough rain. Food and water can become **scarce**. Plants and animals need water to live. Fruits and vegetables cannot grow in a drought. Animals can get sick or die.

1. What is a drought?

   A. when there is too much rain

   B. when there is not enough sunlight

   C. when there is not enough rain

   D. when there is too much snow

2. In a drought, food and water can become ....

   This means there is not enough.

   A. flood

   B. scarce

   C. spoiled

   D. rainy

3. True or false?

   All weather is good for the community.

   A. true

   B. false

Directions: Read the text below. Then answer the questions that follow.

You know that weather can cause changes. Some of these changes are bad for the community. People can also cause bad changes. Look at the chart below.

cause	effect
People throw trash into the river.	There is not enough clean water for people and animals.
People do not care for community plants and trees.	Plants and trees become sick or die.
People waste water.	Water becomes scarce.

1. How can people cause bad changes in the community?

....

....

....

....

....

Directions: Read the text below. Then answer the questions that follow.

"

You know that people cause changes in the community. Remember that some of these changes are bad. Today you will learn ways to make good changes.

The environment is everything around you. Air, water, and plants are part of the environment. People need to care for these things. Here are a few things you can do.

- **Clean up community parks**

- **Never throw trash in rivers, lakes or ponds**

- **Be kind to community animals**

- **Never waste water (turn it off when you are not using it)**

- **Walk or ride your bike (cars and busses can make the air dirty)**

"

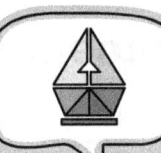
Look at the table below. How can people care for each part of the environment? Write your answer on the right.

plants/animals	
water	
air	

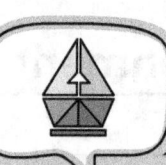
Yesterday you learned about the environment. People must take care of the things around them. Today you will make your own plan. How can you care for your community?

Directions: Read the text below. Then answer the questions that follow.

My Community Care Plan

I, ... (name), will take care of my environment.

First, I will: ....

Then I will: ....

I will also : ....

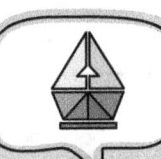
Directions: Read the text below. Then answer the questions that follow.

Zoe and Kim had a picnic at the park. They had sandwiches, water bottles and snacks. After the picnic, they cleaned up. Zoe threw all the trash into the garbage bin. Kim put plastic bottles in the **recycling** bin so they can be used to make new things. Zoe saw a birdbath that was empty. She poured clean water into it. A bird came over to drink from it. Kim and Zoe smiled. Then they walked home.

1. List three ways Zoe and Kim cared for the environment.

....

....

....

2. What is recycling?

....

....

....

Economics

Basic Needs

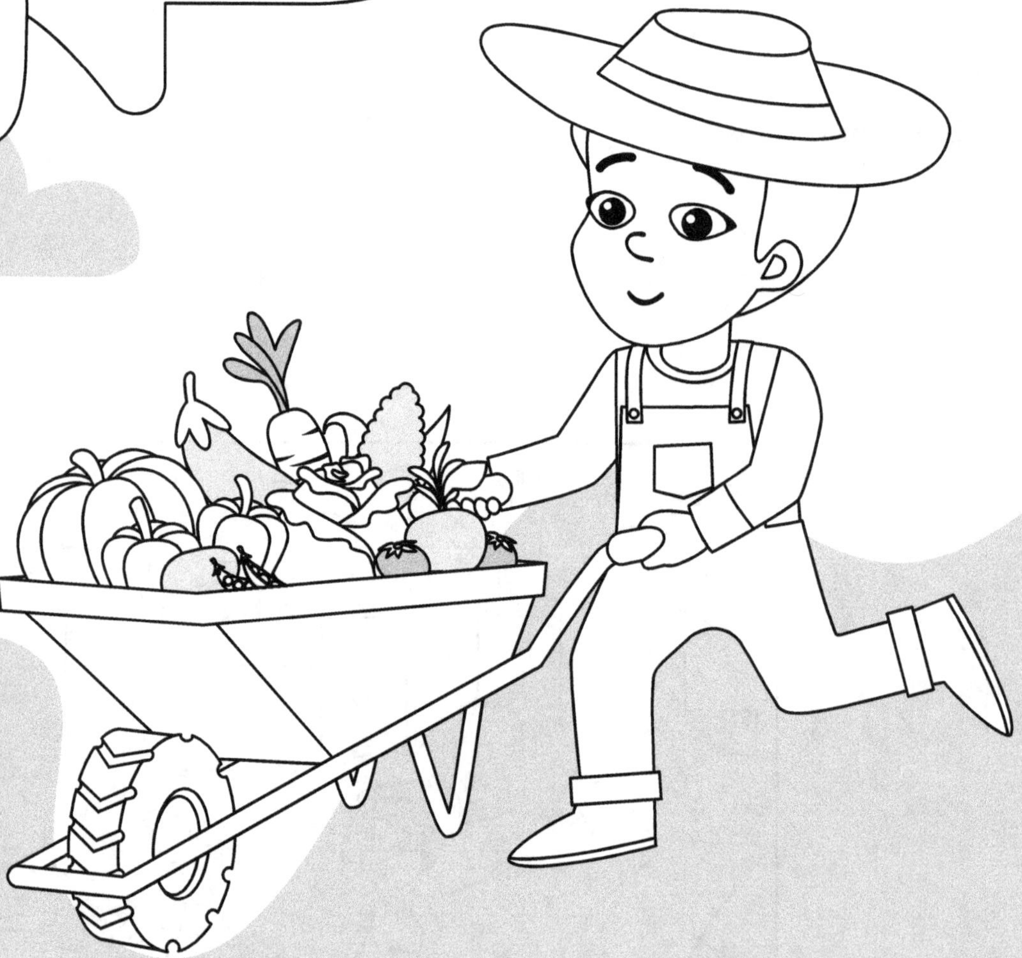

Learn about what people and animals need in order to live on Earth.

ARGOPREP

Directions: Read the text below. Then answer the questions that follow.

> Last week you learned about the environment. These are the things around us. You also learned how to care for the environment. Let's find out why this is important.
>
> You know people and animals need water to live. Plants need water to grow. Living things also need air, food and shelter. These are our **basic needs**. We must protect these things in order to live.

1. What are basic needs?

   A. the things people and animals need to live

   B. the things around us in the community

   C. how people can save the environment

   D. none of these

2. What do people need in order to live?

   A. air

   B. water

   C. shelter

   D. all of these

3. We must .... the things that we need to live.

   A. get rid of

   B. protect

   C. hide

   D. harm

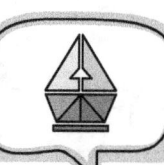
*Yesterday you learned about basic needs. Living things have basic needs. Air, water and shelter are basic needs. Today you will learn about **natural resources**.*

Directions: Read the text below. Then answer the questions that follow.

> Natural resources come from nature. People use them for basic needs. Rivers and lakes are natural resources. They give people water to drink. Trees are also natural resources. People use them for wood. They can use wood to build homes. Trees help keep the air clean, too.

1. What are natural resources?

   A. man-made things that people use

   B. things from nature that people use

   C. types of transportation that people use

   D. bridges and roads that people use

2. Which of these is a natural resource?

   A. mall

   B. bus

   C. river

   D. jacket

3. How can natural resources help people live?

....

....

....

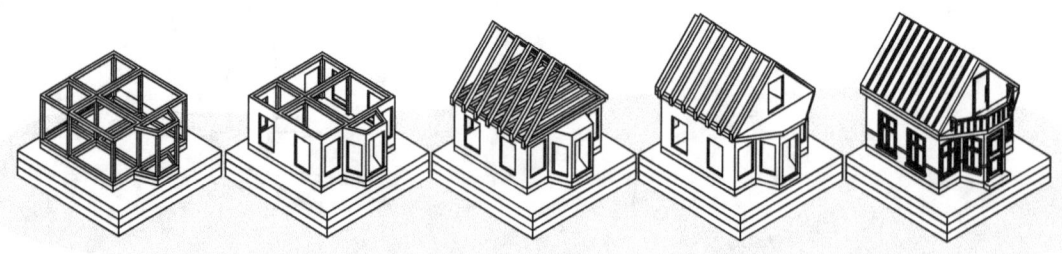

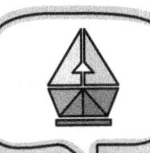
Directions: Read the text below. Then answer the questions that follow.

You know that natural resources help people live. Look at the chart below. It shows natural resources. Think about how people use each one. Write the answer in the box on the right.

Natural Resources	How people use them
soil	
plants	

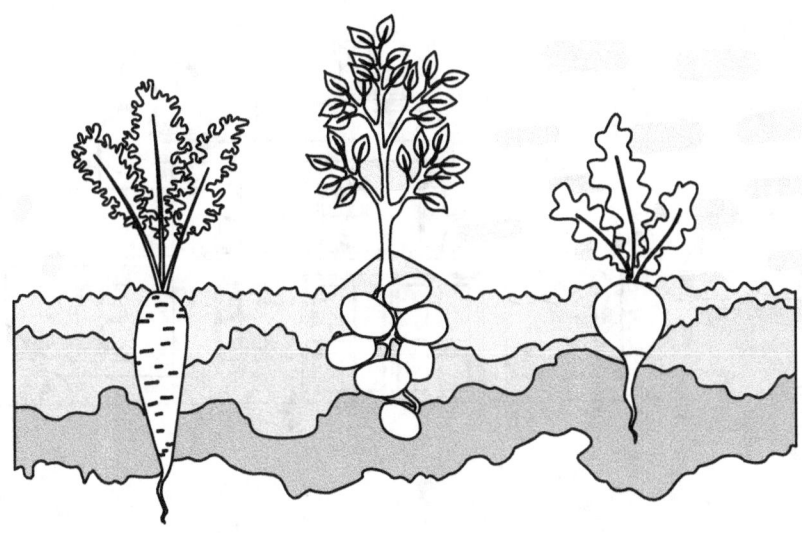

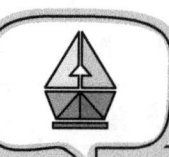
Natural Resources	How people use them
sunlight	
trees	

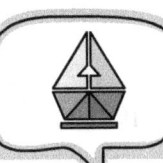
Yesterday you learned about how people use natural resources. Today you will think about what you use every day. How do natural resources help you live?

Directions: Read the text below. Then answer the questions that follow.

1. How do you use water?

....

....

....

....

2. What do you use that comes from trees? Why do you need it?

....

....

....

....

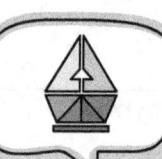
3. Do you eat plants? Where do they come from?

....

....

....

....

....

....

Directions: Read the text below. Then answer the questions that follow.

This week you've learned about basic needs. You also learned about natural resources. People need them in order to live. Today you will label natural resources. Look at the picture below. Write the name of each natural resource in the blank spaces.

Economics

Goods and Services

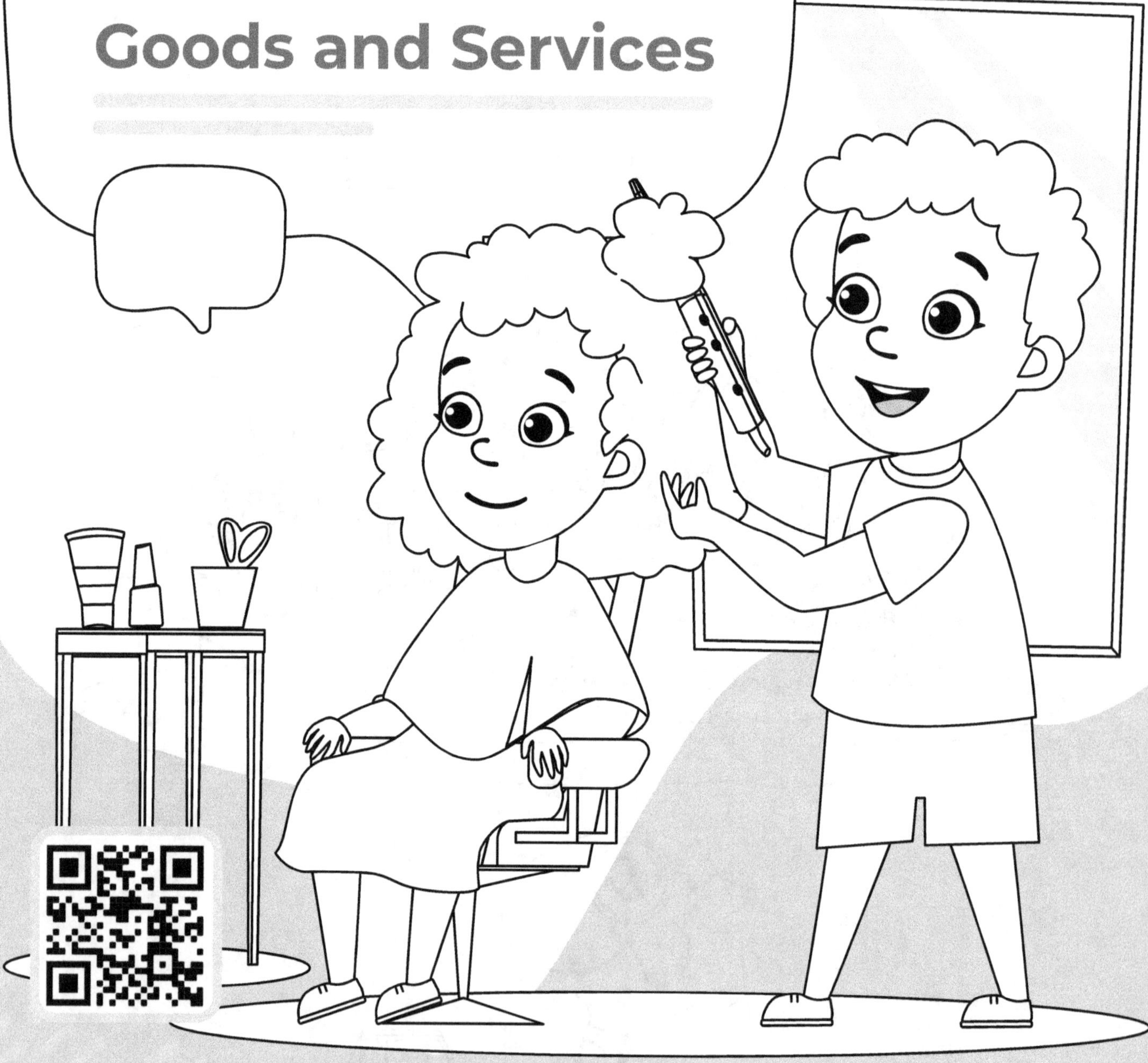

Explore how people meet their basic needs and wants.

ARGOPREP

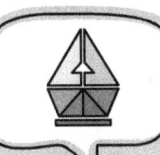
Directions: Read the text below. Then answer the questions that follow.

Last week you learned about basic needs. People need these things to live. There are some things that people want. They can live without these things, but these **wants** can make their lives better.

Have you ever wanted a new toy? You may have really wanted to play with it. It was not something you needed, but it was fun and made you happy. A toy is a want.

1. .... are things that people can live without.

   A. Needs

   B. Resources

   C. Lakes

   D. Wants

2. Which of these is a want?

   A. computer

   B. water

   C. shelter

   D. air

3. Which of these is a need?

   A. sneakers

   B. candy

   C. food

   D. television

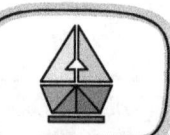
Directions: Read the text below. Then answer the questions that follow.

You know the difference between wants and needs. People need some things to live. They can live without wants.

Think of some wants and needs that people may have. Write them in the table below.

wants	needs

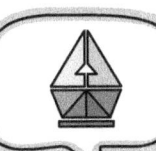
Directions: Read the text below. Then answer the questions that follow.

Remember that people have wants and needs. They find ways to get these things. People shop at stores. They buy **goods** from the store. Goods are things that people use or eat. Clothing, food and tools are goods.

People also buy **services**. A service is something that someone does for you. A barber can cut your hair. Doctors can care for sick people. People use services for their needs and wants.

Look at each picture below. Is it a good or a service? Write the answer on the line.

....

....

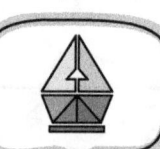
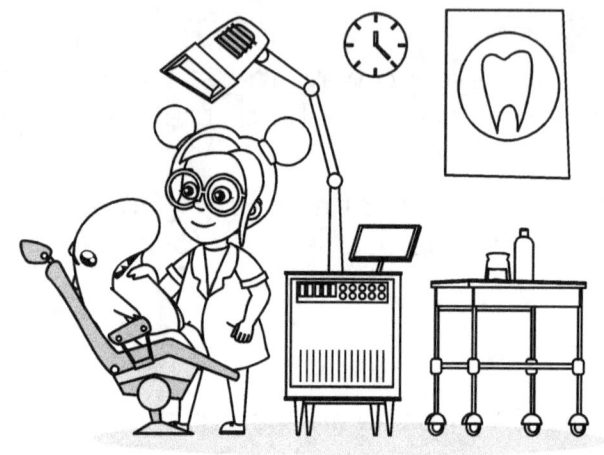

....

....

....

....

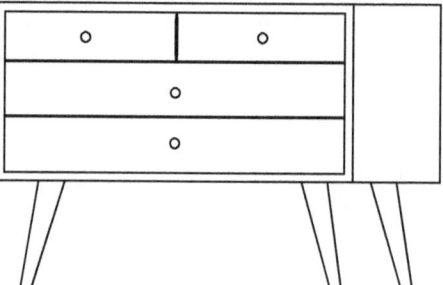

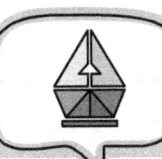
Yesterday you learned about goods and services. Today you will think about goods and services in your community.

Directions: Read the text below. Then answer the questions that follow.

Pretend you are making a shopping list. Write a list of goods that you will buy. Then write a few services that you will buy.

Goods

....

....

....

....

Services

....

....

....

....

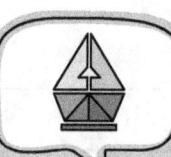
Directions: Read the text below. Then answer the questions that follow.

This week you've learned about needs and wants. You also learned about goods and services. Today you will read about two people. Think about their wants or needs.

1. Kisha went to the hair salon. The hairdresser washed and curled her hair. Was this a need or a want? Did Kisha buy a good or a service?

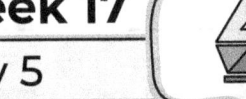
2. Manuel went to the store. He bought chicken, juice and apples. Were these needs or wants? Did Manuel buy goods or a service?

....

....

....

....

Economics
Producers and Consumers

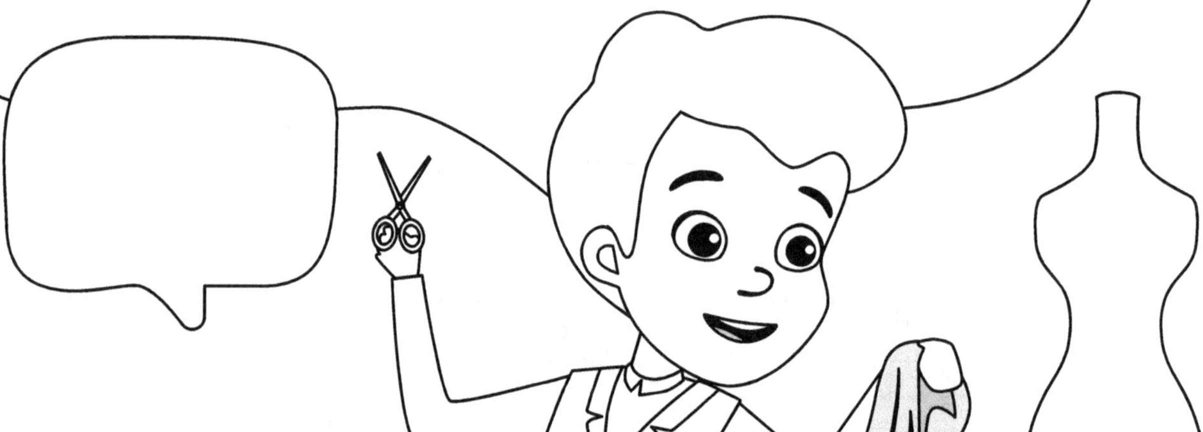

Learn about how people make, sell and buy things.

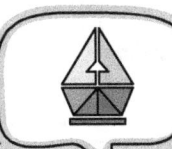
Directions: Read the text below. Then answer the questions that follow.

Last week you learned about goods and services. You know people buy their wants and needs. This week you will learn more about how this works.

> Goods can be made by people. They are then sold to other people. People who make goods are called **producers**. People who buy goods are called **consumers**.

1. What is a producer?

    A. people who buy goods

    B. people who use services

    C. people who make goods

    D. people who have wants

2. Which of these people is a consumer?

    A. a baker that sells cakes

    B. a man who buys a pair of jeans

    C. a baby who wants a stuffed animal

    D. a farmer who sells vegetables

3. True or false?

Consumers buy their wants and needs.

    A. true

    B. false

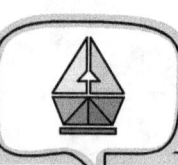
Yesterday you learned about producers and consumers. Producers make goods. Consumers buy them. Today you will learn more about producers.

Directions: Read the text below. Then answer the questions that follow.

You know producers make goods for people to buy. Look at each producer below. What kind of goods do they make?

....

....

....

....

....

....

Directions: Read the text below. Then answer the questions that follow.

Remember that consumers buy goods. Today you will learn about where to buy them.

There are many types of stores. Each store has different types of goods. Which store should you go to? Look at the chart below. Think about what you can buy from each store. Write the answer in the box on the right.

type of store	goods
grocery store	
pet store	

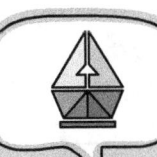

type of store	goods
clothing store	
hardware store	

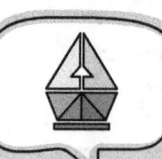
Directions: Read the text below. Then answer the questions that follow.

Pretend you are a producer. You want to open a store in your community. What will you make and sell? Draw a flyer for your new store in the box below.

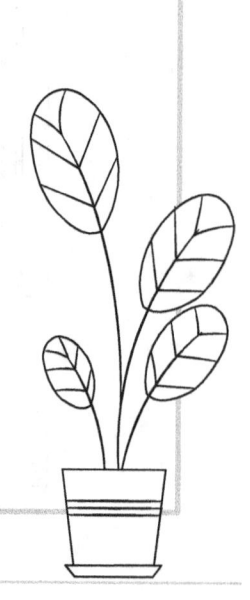

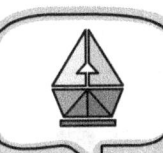
Directions: Read the text below. Then answer the questions that follow.

This week you've learned about producers and consumers. Today you will think about how they work together.

Producers make goods for consumers to buy. Read each step below. Put them in order by number. Write the correct number on the line.

The farmer takes the fruit to the market. ....

People buy fruit from the market. ....

A farmer plants and grows fruit. ....

People take the fruit home to eat. ....

WEEK 19

Economics

Type of Resources

Take a closer look at how people meet their needs through different types of resources.

ARGOPREP

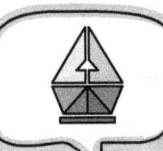
Directions: Read the text below. Then answer the questions that follow.

You've learned that people have needs and wants. They can buy goods and services. You also know producers make things. Consumers buy things.

" Producers are **human resources**. They are people who produce goods and services. They use their skills to do this. A pilot knows how to fly an airplane. He or she is a human resource. People need them in order to ride an airplane. "

1. What are human resources?

   A. people who buy goods and services

   B. people who produce goods and services

   C. places where people buy goods and services

   D. the amount of money people spend on goods and services

2. Who can be a human resource?

   A. a truck

   B. a coat

   C. a teacher

   D. a horse

3. Human resources use their ....

   A. skills

   B. community

   C. consumers

   D. stores

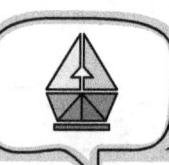
*Yesterday you learned about human resources. Today you will learn about **capital resources**. These are goods that are produced to make other goods. They can also be used to produce services. Human resources need capital resources. A carpenter needs tools to build a house. A producer makes the tools. The carpenter uses them to make things.*

Directions: Read the text below. Then answer the questions that follow.

Look at each human resource. How do they produce goods or services? Think about the capital resources that they need. Write them in the box on the right.

human resource	capital resources
chef	
barber	

human resource	capital resources
plumber	
painter	

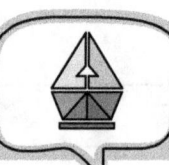
Yesterday you learned about 2 types of resources. You know human resources are people. They produce goods and services. Capital resources are goods. They can be used to make other goods. A few weeks ago, you learned about natural resources which come from nature. People use natural resources for their basic needs.

Directions: Read the text below. Then answer the questions that follow.

Today, you will think about all 3 resources. Look at the resources below. Sort them in the table.

| water | bus driver | hammer |
| computer | nurse | tree |

natural	human	capital

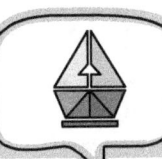
Directions: Read the text below. Then answer the questions that follow.

Think about a human resource in your community. What kind of goods or services do they produce? What type of resources do they use? Write your answers on the line below.

.... are human resources in my community.

They produce goods/services such as ....

....

....

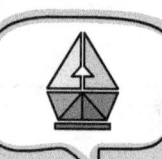
They use capital resources like ....

....

....

They use natural resources like ....

....

....

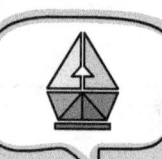

Directions: Read the text below. Then answer the questions that follow.

This week you've learned about types of resources. Today you will answer a few more questions.

1. What are capital resources?

   A. goods that are used to make other goods

   B. goods that are used to make human resources

   C. human resources that produce goods

   D. none of these

2. Which capital resource could be used by a farmer?

   A. an ocean

   B. a rake

   C. a teacher

   D. an oven

3. True or false?

   There are only 2 types of resources.

   A. true

   B. false

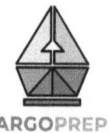

WEEK 20

Economics

Jobs

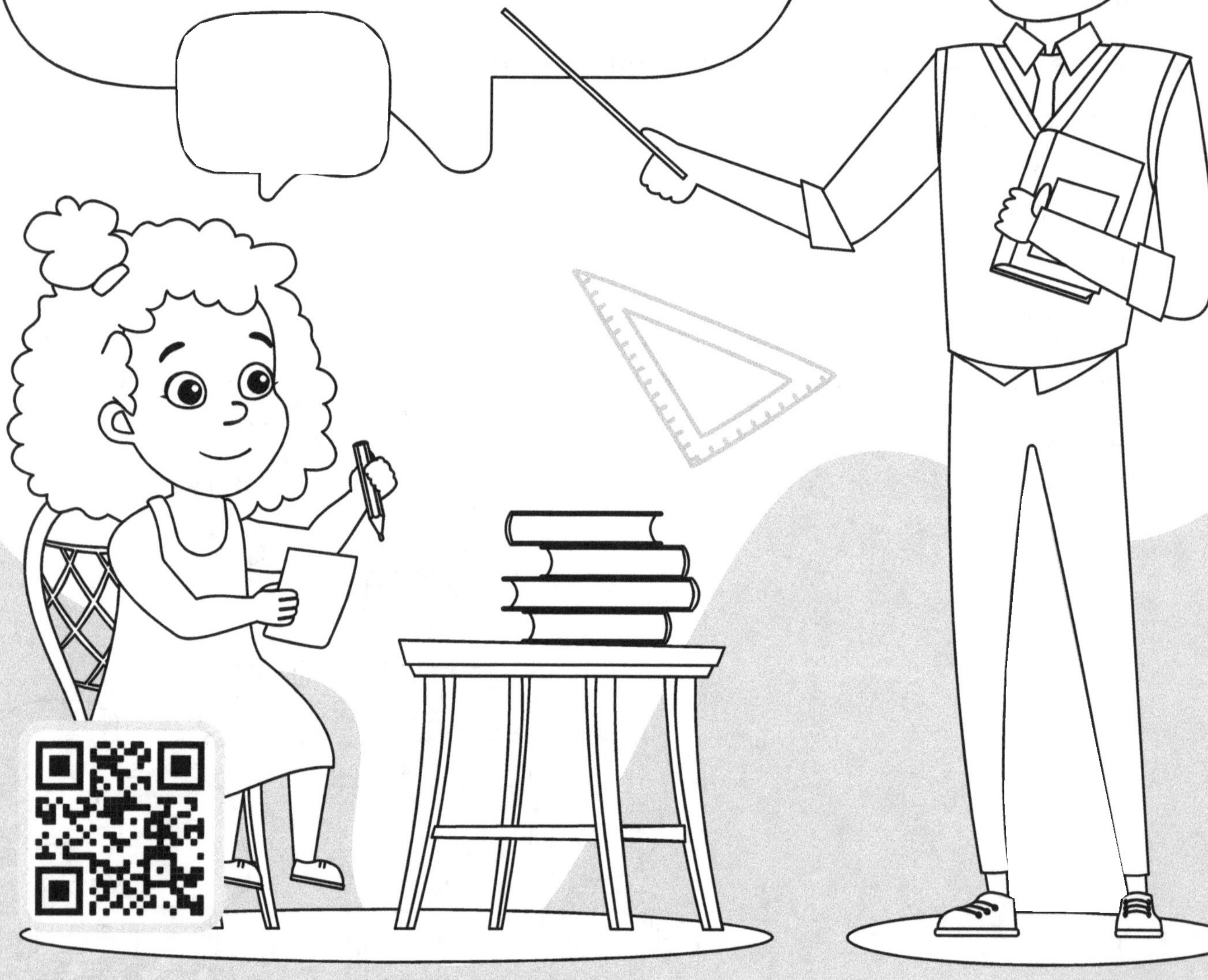

Learn about how people make money to meet their needs.

ARGOPREP

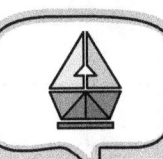
Directions: Read the text below. Then answer the questions that follow.

> Last week you learned about human resources. You know they produce goods and services. Today you will learn about **jobs**. A job is work that people do for money. Human resources get paid for their work. They use their skills to make money.

1. What is a job?

    A. work that people do for fun

    B. a place where people work

    C. work that people do for money

    D. all of these

2. Which of these is a job?

    A. going to bed

    B. working at a store

    C. buying a slice of pizza

    D. washing your pet

3. True or false?

    Human resources have jobs.

    A. true

    B. false

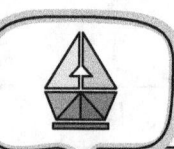
*Yesterday you learned about jobs. Remember that people get paid for jobs. A **hobby** is something that people do for fun. Cooking or playing sports can be a hobby. These things can also be jobs.*

Directions: Read the text below. Then answer the questions that follow.

Read the sentences below. Write *job* or *hobby* on the line.

1. Jonathan cuts grass for his neighbors. They each pay him $10 a week.

....

....

2. Mia loves to sew. She fixed a hole in her mom's blouse.

....

....

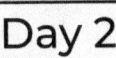
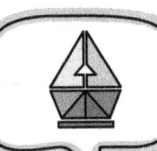

3. Mr. Jones works at a bookstore. He makes $12 an hour.

....

....

4. Lin bakes brownies. She sells them for $1 each.

....

....

5. Will helps his mother wash the dishes. He likes to do chores.

....

....

Directions: Read the text below. Then answer the questions that follow.

You know that people make money from jobs. This money is called **wages**. Some people earn wages per hour. Some jobs may pay people daily or weekly. Look at the job ad below.

HELP WANTED!

Bonnie's Burgers is looking for servers.

Servers will work 5 days a week. You will be paid $50 for each day.

Must take orders and serve food. Servers will also clean tables.

Call Bonnie at 555-1234 for more info.

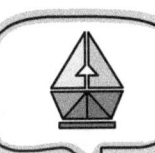
1. What type of job is the ad looking for? What type of work will they do?

....

....

2. What are the daily wages for this job? How much money will be earned every week?

....

....

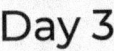

Directions: Read the text below. Then answer the questions that follow.

What type of job would you like to do? Do you want to be a police officer? Would you like to be a singer? Draw a picture of your dream job below.

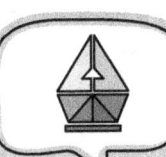
Directions: Read the text below. Then answer the questions that follow.

Remember that human resources have jobs. They can use their jobs to help the community. Look at each job below. What do they do? How does their job help the community? Write your answer on the line.

....

....

....

....

....

....

Answer Sheets

To see the answer key to the entire workbook, you can easily download the answer key from our website!

*Due to the high request from parents and teachers, we have removed the answer key from the workbook so you do not need to rip out the answer key while students work on the workbook.

To watch free video explanations go to: **argoprep.com/social2**
OR scan the QR Code:

Place your mouse over the workbook you have, and you will see the "Download Answers" button.

For detailed video instructions on how to access the "Answer Sheets," please scan this QR code.

Books explanations

All Books   Grade: **All**   Series: **Social Studies**   Search...

7th Grade Social Studies: Daily Practice Workbook

5th Grade Social Studies: Daily Practice Workbook

8th Grade Social Studies: Daily Practice Workbook

4th Grade Social Studies: Daily Practice Workbook

3rd Grade Social Studies: Daily Practice Workbook

2nd Grade Social Studies: Daily Practice Workbook

1st Grade Social Studies: Daily Practice Workbook

Kindergarten Social Studies: Daily Practice Workbook

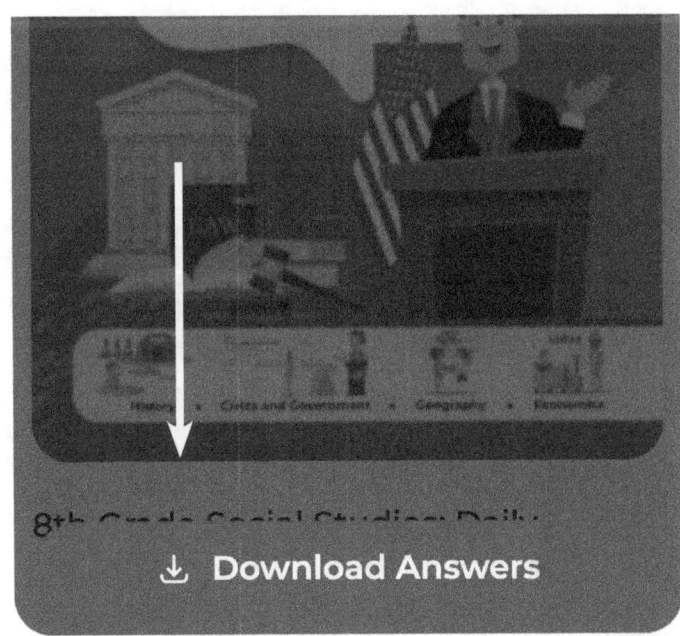

8th Grade Social Studies: Daily

⬇ Download Answers

4th Grade Social Studies: Practice Workbook